HERE COMES
THE
JUDGE

FINDING FREEDOM IN THE PROMISED LAND

HERE COMES
THE
JUDGE

FINDING FREEDOM IN THE PROMISED LAND

G. E. PATTERSON

WHITAKER
HOUSE

Unless otherwise indicated, all Scripture quotations are from the King James Version (KJV) of the Holy Bible.

HERE COMES THE JUDGE

To contact the author:
Bishop G. E. Patterson
Temple of Deliverance, Church of God in Christ
369 G. E. Patterson Avenue
Memphis, Tennessee 38126
(901) 521-9160
Web site: www.bbless.org

ISBN: 0-88368-775-5
Printed in the United States of America
© 2002 by G. E. Patterson

Whitaker House
30 Hunt Valley Circle
New Kensington, PA 15068
web site: www.whitakerhouse.com

Library of Congress Cataloging-in-Publication Data (pending)

1 2 3 4 5 6 7 8 9 10 11 12 13 14 / 11 10 09 08 07 06 05 04 03 02

Contents

Introduction

Convicted...Sentenced... Set Free!

Are you enjoying all of God's blessings in your life today?

Are you receiving the fullness of God's promises?

Are you dwelling in total protection and provision—spirit, mind, body, relationships, material possessions?

Are you experiencing the love and presence of God in your life, without any hindrances of fear, doubt, or other emotional need?

In other words, are you living in freedom?

If your answer is anything but a clear and resounding "yes," then you are not living in the Land of Abundance and Blessing that God has prepared for you, called you to, and promised to you as His beloved child.

If you cannot answer "yes," then in all likelihood, you aren't simply doing without the fullness of God's blessing, but you are under attack or oppression in some area of your life. You are living

7

in a state of being convicted and sentenced. You are imprisoned spiritually and emotionally, which is even more serious than being imprisoned physically.

I have good news for you if you are living in a state of being convicted and sentenced—God desires to deliver you and set you free! He wants you to be free of whatever is holding you back from entering into His joy, peace, provision, protection, and infinitely loving presence!

Not only does God desire to save you and fill you with His Holy Spirit, He also desires to give you a place—and a purpose—on this earth. In order to help you occupy that place fully—and fulfill that purpose fully—He has a specific plan for your deliverance and your victory over the evil that has you shackled and bound.

Let me ask you several vitally important questions: Are you willing to move forward to claim all that God has promised to you in His Word? Are you willing to be set free? Are you sick and tired of being sick and tired—are you fed up with not having all that God has promised you, to the point where you are willing to start living your life God's way in order to receive God's best?

"Of course!" you may say. But don't answer too quickly.

You see, responsibilities come with freedom. Choices are more abundant with freedom. Decisions are often less clear with freedom. Obedience must become an act of your own will when you live in freedom.

Being genuinely and completely set free requires your willingness to do whatever it takes to become a genuine, fully submitted, one-hundred-percent dedicated follower of Jesus Christ. Are you not only willing to declare with your lips that Jesus is Lord, but also to obey with your life the leading of the Holy Spirit? Are you willing to accept *all* the challenges of being set free?

Those are the questions that are at the heart of this book.

I

Our Vulnerability to Attack

A t the very outset of this book, let me make one thing very clear: Enemies don't need an excuse to attack. They just attack.

Some enemies attack out of malice; some out of boredom; some with a strong intent to steal, kill, or destroy us; and some with a spur-of-the-moment impulse to take advantage of a situation they perceive might boost their power, wealth, or status. Furthermore, enemies usually attack us when we are least expecting them and feel most vulnerable.

What is true of our earthly, human enemies is also true of our enemies in the spiritual realm. The devil is the archenemy of our souls. He never ceases to be our enemy, no matter how mature we grow in our faith or how strong we are in the Spirit. He is our enemy until the moment we die and enter the presence of the Lord in paradise.

We must recognize also that the devil is not omnipotent (all-powerful), omniscient (all-knowing and all-wise), or omnipresent (capable of being in all time and space at once). Those infinite terms belong solely to God.

The devil is a created being—just like all other created beings, both earthly and spiritual—with a finite capacity, a finite ability, a finite territory, a limited time span in which to work, and a limited number of demons under his control (those demons being outnumbered two-to-one by God's holy angels). We must never give the devil more power than he already has. He is not on equal footing with God—not now, not ever, no matter how hard he has tried through the ages. He'll lie and tell us otherwise, but that's his very nature—he is a liar and the father of all who lie.

While we recognize the devil's limitations, we also must recognize that he is more powerful than we are as human beings when we operate in our own strength. The devil knows more than any individual human being, has greater spiritual and natural power, and is not bound by a physical body. Without the Holy Spirit filling your being, you are no match for the devil. However, with the Holy Spirit filling you, you are "more than a conqueror." (See Romans 8:37.) Thank you Jesus

Finally, we must recognize that the devil is forever on the prowl against us—he is an evil adversary, a wicked foe who constantly and relentlessly seeks our demise.

The Bible describes the devil as *"a roaring lion...seeking whom he may devour"* (1 Pet. 5:8). Just as a shaggy, powerful lion stalks its prey, the devil seeks the weakest, most vulnerable, and often the most innocent in any community. In your life, he will attack you at your weakest moment and in your weakest area. He will seek to attack you when you are already feeling discouraged, exhausted, lonely, abused, or ill-used by others, down-hearted, weary of life, or emotionally "whipped." The devil especially attacks those who don't seem to be able to defend themselves, including those who are not connected to Jesus Christ in a strong way. Among those who believe in Jesus Christ, he will seek out those who are living in disobedience and sin, those who are straying from what they know to be the right way to live, and those who aren't in close fellowship with the Lord.

Occasionally the devil will launch an all-out assault on a true Holy Spirit-filled believer who is strong in faith and is living in purity, holiness, and righteousness. But in the overall scheme of things, the percentages fall to those who are weak, vulnerable, and spiritually disconnected from God. They are the "easiest pickin's" for the devil.

Have You Made Yourself Vulnerable?

Now what does all this have to do with our living in the fullness and freedom of God's blessings, which includes total deliverance from our enemy?

The fact is, a significant percentage of those of us who call ourselves Christians have made ourselves spiritually vulnerable and weak. We have unlocked the door of our souls and opened it a few inches to allow easy access to the devil and all of his evil minions and schemes.

We are not alone in that. The Israelites of old did the same thing. They adopted spiritual practices and were in a spiritual state that made them highly vulnerable to enemy attack. Not many years after entering the Promised Land, they began to rely solely on their own ability to defeat their neighboring enemies. They turned away from God, became spiritually weak, and, in so doing, opened themselves to severe attack.

Now, the Israelites never ceased to be God's chosen people. Rather, they had ceased to worship the one, true, and living God as their chosen deity. Some of us today call ourselves Christians—we are saved and filled with God's Holy Spirit—but we are no longer worshipping the one, true, and living Lord with our whole heart, mind, and soul. Something has taken root in us that has drawn us away from Him, and the result has been vulnerability to attack and oppression from the enemy.

Just as God desired to deliver the Israelites, He desires to deliver us. *It is so*

Just as God required certain things of the Israelites, He requires certain things of us. *It is so*

Just as God poured out the anointing of His Spirit to bring freedom for His people, He pours out His anointing on us today. *It is so*

In studying the Israelites, we can learn a great deal about why we are in the state we are in today—and how God seeks to deliver us so we might live fully and freely in His blessings.

In the case of the Israelites, things went dramatically downhill spiritually after the death of Joshua.

The Legacy of Joshua

Most people who have ever read the Bible or ever attended Sunday school know the name of Joshua—he's the one we associate from early childhood with the conquest of Jericho when "the walls came a' tumblin' down." At the time the Israelites entered the Promised Land, Joshua was their God-appointed leader.

Joshua was one of the twelve men whom Moses sent to spy out the land of Canaan. Ten of the spies returned saying, *"We be not able to go up against the people; for they are stronger than we"* (Num. 13:31). Only Joshua aligned himself with Caleb who said, *"Let us go up at once, and possess it; for we are well able to overcome it"* (Num. 13:30). Joshua tore his clothing as a sign of mourning when the Israelites refused to trust God and chose instead to fear the giants they saw in Canaan. (See Numbers 13–14.)

In his younger years, Joshua had been the "administrative and personal assistant" to Moses. He had accompanied Moses when Moses went up the mountain to receive the commandments engraved on stone from the hand of God—he didn't go all the way to the top of the mountain, but he's the only one of the Israelites, several million strong at that time, who was chosen to make part of that journey with Moses. (See Exodus 24:13.)

Joshua—this great man of faith and service—was the one God chose to succeed Moses and to lead the children of Israel across the Jordan River into the Promised Land after forty years of wandering in the wilderness. (See Numbers 27:18–23.)

A String of Victories at God's Command

The generation that entered Canaan under Joshua accomplished a great deal in taking the land as God commanded. They scored important victories at strategic sites. As you read through the book of Joshua, you'll find that it is a book of one victory after another. The Israelites took Jericho and the city of Ai. They defeated the Amorites, Hittites, Perizzites, Jebusites, and Hivites in key battles. We read in God's Word:

So Joshua took all that land, the hills, and all the south country, and all the land of Goshen, and the valley, and the plain, and the mountain of Israel, and the valley of the same; even from the mount Halak, that goeth up to Seir, even unto Baalgad in the valley of Lebanon under mount Hermon: and all their kings he took, and smote them, and slew them. Joshua made war a long time with all those kings. There was not a city that made peace with the children of Israel, save the Hivites the inhabitants of Gibeon: all other they took in battle. (Josh. 11:16–19)

And note the verse that follows:

For it was of the LORD to harden their hearts, that they should come against Israel in battle, that he might destroy them utterly, and that they might have no favour, but that he might destroy them, as the LORD commanded Moses. (v. 20) *Note this important*

A key pattern is established again and again—the Lord spoke to Joshua about where to fight, how to fight, and when to fight. And as Joshua and the people under his command obeyed the Lord, God gave the victory. *Yaay halleluah!*

The Lord, however, did not hand the Land of Promise to the Israelites on a silver platter—they had to fight for it. The milk and honey promised to them didn't get served in beautiful serving bowls. They had to conquer their enemies to receive this fullness of blessing. As they fought for the land with their faith and trust in God, they were doing what God had told them to do—and their victory was assured. *My faith & trust is in the Lord*

This is a critical point for us to recognize in our own lives.

God's pattern for winning a battle is this—for the Israelites, for all God's people through the ages, and for you and me:

Is it a

1. Hear from God. We must hear from God that He wants us to take possession of a specific territory, which may be an area of our lives, a habit, a business, or a piece of land—things both physical and spiritual. *?*

2. Make God the General of the Battle. We must know that the battle is ultimately the Lord's and the Lord is the author of our victory plan. What good is a battle plan unless it is truly a "victory" plan? None of us wants to fight a battle we lose! *My God is the Commander*

3. Fight the Battle. We must do the fighting. There's something in the battle that is our part. *What's my part*

Certainly God sent His miracles again and again to help Joshua and the Israelites. The walls of Jericho came down in a supernatural way. The sun stood still in the valley of Ajalon—a miracle never witnessed before or since the Lord revealed the sin of Achan in a sovereign way. The miracles were there—but the people still had to fight.

The taking of the land was a joint effort: The people of God did what they could do and what they were told to do; God did for the people what only He could do, and that was to secure for them a definitive victory.

In Joshua 11:23 we read, *"So Joshua took the whole land, according to all that the LORD said unto Moses; and Joshua gave it*

*for an inheritance unto Israel according to their divisions by their
tribes. And the land rested from war."*

And Then...Another Generation Arose

The borders of the inheritance were secured under Joshua,
almost like the outline of a drawing that had yet to be colored in.
However, the complete taking and occupying of the land was still
to be done.

But then, Joshua died. And the Bible tells us that "another generation arose." Things changed.

We read in God's Word:

*And when Joshua had let the people go, the children of Israel
went every man unto his inheritance to possess the land.
And the people served the LORD all the days of Joshua, and
all the days of the elders that outlived Joshua, who had seen
all the great works of the LORD, that he did for Israel. And
Joshua, the son of Nun, the servant of the LORD, died, being
an hundred and ten years old. And they buried him in the
border of his inheritance in Timnathheres, in the mount of
Ephraim, on the north side of the hill Gaash. And also all that
generation were gathered unto their fathers: and there arose
another generation after them, which knew not the LORD, nor
yet the works which he had done for Israel.* (Judg. 2:6–10)

The word *"and"* punctuates this passage like the ticking of a
great and fateful clock. Time passes. Eventually, Joshua sent the
tribes to their allotted areas to "inherit" the rest of the territory—in
other words, to take full control over it.

As long as Joshua and the elders of that generation were alive,
the people served the Lord. We might call that generation the conquering generation—they were the leaders of the people who had
crossed the Jordan River out of the wilderness and who claimed
the territory for God.

Then Joshua died.

They buried him in his rightful place of inheritance.

All the people of the conquering generation died and the next generation did not know the Lord. They didn't know what God required of them or had promised to them. They didn't follow the traditions and laws that their fathers had kept faithfully.

And more specifically, they broke the foremost of all the commandments God had given them. They no longer kept the one commandment of God that ensured their relationship with Him and their full provision, protection, and freedom.

2

The Supreme Commandment: Worship God Only

G od's commandments do not change. The commandments brought down by Moses from Mount Sinai were just as much in effect in Joshua's day as they were in the days before Joshua's leadership. They are just as much in effect today.

The first words that Moses spoke to the Israelites after his encounter with God were these:

> *And God spake all these words, saying, I am the* Lord *thy God, which have brought thee out of the land of Egypt, out of the house of bondage. Thou shalt have no other gods before me. Thou shalt not make unto thee any graven image, or any likeness of any thing that is in heaven above, or that is in the earth beneath, or that is in the water under the earth: Thou shalt not bow down thyself to them, nor serve them: for I the* Lord *thy God am a jealous God, visiting the iniquity of the fathers upon the children unto the third and fourth generation of them that hate me; and showing mercy unto thousands of them that love me, and keep my commandments.* (Exod. 20:1–6)

17

Here Comes the Judge

The first two of the Ten Commandments are still the first two of the Ten Commandments. God has never withdrawn these commands, countered these commands, or superceded these commands. The first two of the Ten Commandments are absolutes.

All the Israelites under Moses knew these commandments. These commandments, along with the other commandments of God, were so important that God reminded Joshua of them at the time Joshua took the reins of leadership from Moses.

Shortly after Joshua became the head of the Israelites, God said this to him:

> As I was with Moses, so I will be with thee: I will not fail thee, nor forsake thee. Be strong and of a good courage: for unto this people shalt thou divide for an inheritance the land, which I sware unto their fathers to give them. Only be thou strong and very courageous, that thou mayest observe to do according to all the law, which Moses my servant commanded thee: turn not from it to the right hand or to the left, that thou mayest prosper whithersoever thou goest. This book of the law shall not depart out of thy mouth; but thou shalt meditate therein day and night, that thou mayest observe to do according to all that is written therein: for then thou shalt make thy way prosperous, and then thou shalt have good success. Have not I commanded thee? Be strong and of a good courage; be not afraid, neither be thou dismayed: for the LORD thy God is with thee whithersoever thou goest. (Josh. 1:5–9)

God's command to Joshua had two parts: Be strong in spirit (courageous), and observe all the law.

The two must always go together. It takes courage to keep the law. The law tells us what to do so we can take courage in knowing we are doing the right thing.

God told Joshua to keep all the law and not turn to the left or right. No detours! No straying! No substitutions!

The Supreme Commandment: Worship God Only

Joshua was to speak only what he had learned from the law. He was to meditate on the law day and night. "*Meditate*" didn't mean only to think about the law, which is how we tend to define the word. It meant to repeat something to your own mind and speak it out of your own lips continually so that what you were meditating on became ingrained on your heart. People who meditated in that time often looked and sounded as if they were muttering to themselves. They were repeating verses of the law by memory, reciting the commandments to their own minds in such a way that their ears heard the words. It's difficult to get into error if you are thinking and speaking God's Word to your mind during every waking moment possible—filling your mind, heart, and ears with God's Word every moment you aren't working on a task that requires your total concentration, speaking to someone else, or writing something.

Joshua was commanded to make the law his very way of thinking so it would automatically become his way of speaking and acting in any given situation.

Look at God's promise at what would happen if Joshua was courageous and observed all the law. The Lord said, "*Thou shalt make thy way prosperous*" and "*thou shalt have good success*" (v. 8). God wanted Joshua to have *all* his needs met—spiritually, mentally, emotionally, relationally, financially, and materially. He wanted him to prosper—not just live a notch above the poverty level. He wanted him to have good success—to lead successfully and take the land successfully.

Let me ask you, "What more could you possibly want?"

Every person I know wants to experience the fullness of God's prosperity, which covers all aspects of a person's life. Every person I know wants to succeed at the work he or she does and be an influence for good in the lives of other people. Every person I know wants to live in total emotional and spiritual freedom.

Joshua didn't have any reservation, hesitation, or compromise. He obeyed.

And as Joshua led the people, they followed.

As Joshua listened to God's voice, God gave battle plans. *form*

I will have

As the battles were fought, God gave victory after victory.

What does the Lord ask of you? The very same things He asked of Joshua: to be courageous and to keep all His command-ments. In every battle you ever find yourself, God requires these two things of you personally:

1. Courage to face your enemy and fight.

2. Obedience to God's commandments—not only in lip service, but in your thought life and all aspects of your behavior. *behavior think & speak matters to you Lord*

It's not enough just to be courageous. You have to obey.

It isn't enough just to obey in your heart. You must have the courage to obey in *all* your actions. *only through Jesus*

Make the Choice to Worship God

Just as Joshua had been challenged and commanded by God, so Joshua challenged and commanded the Israelites:

Now therefore fear the LORD, and serve him in sincerity and in truth: and put away the gods which your fathers served on the other side of the flood, and in Egypt; and serve ye the LORD. And if it seem evil unto you to serve the LORD, choose you this day whom ye will serve; whether the gods which your fathers served that were on the other side of the flood, or the gods of the Amorites, in whose land ye dwell: but as for me and my house, we will serve the LORD. And the people answered and said, God forbid that we should forsake the LORD, to serve other gods; for the LORD our God, he it is that brought us up and our fathers out of the land of Egypt, from the house of bondage, and which did those great signs in our sight, and preserved us in all the way wherein we went, and among all the people through whom we passed: and

> the LORD drave out from before us all the people, even the
> Amorites which dwelt in the land: therefore will we also
> serve the LORD; for he is our God.   (Josh. 24:14–18)

Joshua was not speaking to infidels. He was speaking to God's chosen people—the most blessed people on earth at that time. He was speaking to a people that had seen God part the Jordan River so they could walk across it on dry ground. They had seen God cause a city wall to crack apart and tumble at the sound of their shouts and blasts of their trumpets. They had seen God provide for them in battle after battle. They had witnessed a day in which the sun stood still so they could fight a battle to its victorious conclusion.

And yet Joshua said, *"Choose you this day, whom ye will serve."* I serve father God Jesus 'the holy spirit'

God asks the same question of you and me.

Our choice for Jesus is not just a choice we make on the day we are saved. It's a choice we make every day of our lives. It's a forever choice, and it is a "this hour" choice. The choice to worship God only is a choice we are called to make continually...constantly ...consistently.

Countless Christians have experienced the presence and power of God only to wander off in search of something that captured their imagination or pricked their curiosity. Countless Christians have known what it means to walk in the power of the Holy Spirit and to see great miracles from the hand of God only to be enticed by a temptation to fall away into sin.   3-4-24

Have you made your choice today for Jesus Christ? Yes

Have you decided in your heart, mind, and will that Jesus is the only way, truth, and life? (See John 14:6.) Yes 6:37pm

You need to stand on that conviction, regardless of any ill winds that blow or your inability to understand certain circumstances that hit your life.

The decision you make regarding Jesus, which establishes your relationship with God, is the foremost decision you will ever make regarding your future—not only your eternal future, but also your future in the days remaining for you on this earth. It is the decision that makes all the difference in your receiving God's blessings and living in the fullness and freedom of the promises He has made to you.

A Repeating of Moses' Words...

In challenging the Israelites to make a sell-out choice for God, Joshua wasn't stating anything new. In many ways, he was repeating the words of Moses—a message that had spelled out what the people could and should expect when they entered the Promised Land. This message, given near the end of Moses' life, was a message that clearly outlined the need for the Israelites to make an ongoing commitment to worshipping God only:

That thou mightest fear the LORD thy God, to keep all his statutes and his commandments, which I command thee, thou, and thy son, and thy son's son, all the days of thy life; and that thy days may be prolonged. Hear therefore, O Israel, and observe to do it; that it may be well with thee, and that ye may increase mightily, as the LORD God of thy fathers hath promised thee, in the land that floweth with milk and honey. Hear, O Israel: The LORD our God is one LORD: and thou shalt love the LORD thy God with all thine heart, and with all thy soul, and with all thy might. And these words, which I command thee this day, shall be in thine heart: and thou shalt teach them diligently unto thy children, and shalt talk of them when thou sittest in thine house, and when thou walkest by the way, and when thou liest down, and when thou risest up. And thou shalt bind them for a sign upon thine hand, and they shall be as frontlets between thine eyes. And thou shalt write them upon the posts of thy house, and on thy gates. And it shall be, when the LORD thy God shall have brought thee into the land which he sware unto thy fathers, to Abraham, to Isaac, and to Jacob, to give thee great and goodly cities, which thou buildedst not, and houses full of all good things, which thou filledst not, and wells digged, which thou diggedst not, vineyards and olive trees, which thou plantedst not; when thou shalt have eaten and be full; then beware lest thou forget the LORD, which brought thee forth out of the land of Egypt, from the house of bondage. Thou shalt fear the LORD thy God, and serve him, and shalt swear by his name. Ye shall not go after other gods, of the gods of the people which are round about you; (For the LORD thy God is a jealous God among you) lest the anger of the LORD thy God be kindled against thee, and destroy thee from off the face of the earth. Ye shall not tempt the LORD your God, as ye tempted him in Massah. Ye shall diligently keep the commandments of the LORD your God, and his testimonies, and his statutes, which he hath commanded thee. And thou shalt do that which is right and good in the sight of the LORD: that it may be well with thee, and that thou mayest go in and possess the good land which the LORD sware unto thy fathers, to cast out all thine enemies from before thee, as the LORD hath spoken. (Deut. 6:2–19)

Let me point out several key truths from this passage.

Expected to Obey

First, the Lord made it very clear that He expected His people to keep His commandments, statutes, and judgments. They were to know and revere God's laws in their hearts—the law was to take root deep within them so that it would never leave their thinking.

Beyond revering God's commandments in their hearts, they were also to actually *do* what God had said to do. They were to make God's commandments the rule of their homes. They were to keep every aspect of their coming and going, their doing and speaking, in line with God's commandments.

Expected to Teach

Second, God expected His people to teach these commandments, statutes, and judgments to their heirs. They were to teach them all the days of their lives so their children and grandchildren might also revere and do what God had said to do.

The Israelites were not only to teach the commandments by repeating them or by sermons, but they were also to teach them by the example of their lives. In other words, the children would learn by watching their parents keep the commandments, speak about the commandments, and show in their lives how the commandments were to be lived out day by day.

Expected to Love God

Third, God expected His people not only to keep His commandments, but also to love Him with a singleness of devotion. They were to love Him with their heart, soul, and might—in other words, their will (heart), their emotions (soul), and their physical and material acts of worship (might). They were to love God not merely as an emotion of their heart, but as the very motivation for all they did.

Blessing Based upon Obedience

Keeping the commandments was the key for the Israelites to experience blessing and increase in their lives. God's great promise for keeping His commandments and loving Him with their whole lives was very practical—a land flowing with milk and honey! This meant that the land God had for them would have pastures so lush that the cattle would be able to produce an abundance of milk, and the flowers and foliage would be so lush that the pollen from the blossoms would cause the honey bees to produce an abundance of honey.

God didn't stop there, however! He promised to give them *"houses full of all good things,"* wells for water, vineyards, and olive trees. This is all a way of saying that God's people were going to have plenty of the very best that life had to offer in the material realm if they kept His commandments, taught His commandments to their children, and loved Him with all their beings.

With these very positive statements of expectation and bless-ing, God also issues a warning. WARNING

God described Himself as being jealous for His people—in other words, He wanted the love and obedience of the people who were rightfully His. And He warned that those who turned to other gods would experience His anger and would face destruction.

We are just like the Israelites in so many ways! God knows human nature. He knows that those who begin to enjoy a bless-ing often forget Him. As a pastor, I see it time and time again—the spiritual commitment of some people declines when things start going well for them. They seem to forget that God is the One who gave them the blessings they are enjoying. They start to think that they have done something on their own, rather than rejoicing that God has enabled them to succeed. God warned very strongly against this tendency.

Moses called the people to keep the commandments of God *"diligently"* and to *"do that which is right and good"* in the Lord's eyes so they might go in and possess the good land and cast out all their enemies.

Has any of this changed in the centuries that have passed?

Not a word of it!

This is what God says to us today. He requires our total obe-dience to His commands, and specifically to His supreme com-mand: Have no other gods. Obey and love God *only.*

It isn't enough that we are saved and sanctified and filled with the Holy Spirit. God calls us to obey His commandments, and to do so without any reservation, hesitation, or compromise.

Let's focus on those three words for a moment:

Reservation

Do you truly believe that all God's commandments apply to you today? Do you find yourself trying to make excuses or offer justifications for various commandments that you aren't sure are worth the time and effort to be obeyed? That's reservation. God wants us to fully embrace His commandments.

Some people have reservations about God's commandments because they see them as stifling their fun or inhibiting their personal style. Neither is actually true! God's commandments are for our benefit. What may seem like emotional fun at the moment rarely turns out to be enjoyable in the long run. Instead of having fun, our breaking God's commandments is actually inviting pain. Begin to see God's commandments as being for your benefit and you'll likely get rid of your reservations about obeying them.

Hesitation

When you hear the words *obey* or *commandment,* do you suddenly want to turn tail and run? Do you pause if asked the question, "Do you always seek to obey God?" That's hesitation. God expects us to obey quickly when He commands us to do something. We should be eager to obey.

Some people hesitate in obeying God's commands because they aren't quite sure they have heard God's voice or they aren't quite sure they understand the commandment they've read in the Bible. (In all likelihood, they understand what God means when He says "thou shalt not"—they just don't want to obey that command so they say they don't understand it.) If you genuinely aren't sure you've heard God or understand the Bible correctly, ask somebody who knows how to hear God's voice and who does understand the Bible. When you get confirmation about what is required of you before the Lord, don't hesitate any longer—obey!

Compromise

Do you ever try to strike a bargain with God, saying, "I'll do this if You won't require me to do that"? Do you ever say to yourself, "Well, I'll obey this commandment to the minimum requirement—I'll get by with as little obedience as possible"? That's compromise.

Some people compromise because they aren't really sure they want to be Christians. Oh, they want to go to heaven when they die...they just don't want to live for Christ until the day they die. They don't want any persecution, rejection, or loss of status for standing up for Christ and obeying Him fully in their day-to-day walk. They want to do only the politically correct thing so they can appear tolerant in all ways and gain the respect of ungodly people. Jesus said plainly,

> *Whosoever therefore shall confess me before men, him will I confess also before my Father which is in heaven. But whosoever shall deny me before men, him will I also deny before my Father which is in heaven.* (Matt. 10:32–33)

Settle your relationship with Christ once and for all. Live for Him! Refuse to compromise with the world, the flesh, or the devil.

The prophet Joel said, *"Multitudes, multitudes in the valley of decision: for the day of the LORD is near in the valley of decision"* (Joel 3:14). God's response to you is based on your decisions regarding Him and His commandments. What is your choice?

Pass It On!

Not only do we have a responsibility to obey God's commandments, but we also have a responsibility to teach God's commandments and judgments to our children, and until they are of legal age, we are to require them to obey God's commandments. We are to train them to obey. (See Proverbs 22:6.) To train is to build up habits of thinking, speaking, and behaving. It is to run the drills of obedience to certain principles again and again so that doing the right thing before God is an automatic impulse.

Even after your children are adults, you have a responsibility to be a person who holds your children accountable for their choices and behavior.

Never give a reward for disobedience.

Never wink at sin.

God doesn't. *Do this Its Crucil*

Single-Hearted Devotion

The first great commandment of both the Old and New Testaments is to love God with all your heart, mind, and soul. What you love, you cherish, you make time for, you honor, you respect, and you sacrifice to maintain.

How much do you value your relationship with God ? How much do you value the fact that you have been saved, purchased by the shed blood of Jesus Christ on an old rugged cross at Calvary?

Are you devoted to the Lord?

Do you desire His approval, His presence, His power, and His grace more than anything else in life?

Breaking or Keeping?

It is in the power of each one of us to choose to break or keep God's commandments. It is within our power to choose to be devoted to the Lord with our whole life. *help me lord*

Important note for God makes it very clear: Keep My commandments fully and you will be in a position to receive absolutely every one of My blessings. I will defend you. I will reward you. I will make certain that you have all that you need, when you need it.

God also makes it very clear: Stop loving Me wholeheartedly and stop keeping My commandments, and I will turn away from you. You will not be able to count on Me to defeat your enemies or bless you. You will have taken yourself out of the realm of My blessing and abundance.

Will God disown you? No. You are His. He will still be your God. He will still call you His child.

But will God do anything to overlook or bless your sin? Never.

Our

God cannot tolerate sin. It is one hundred percent opposite His nature. He cannot dwell in the presence of sin.

To choose to worship other gods is to breach your relationship with God. It is to open yourself up to all kinds of agony and suffering.

I choose you PapaGod in Jesus name thank you holy spirit

God's Tough-Love Approach

Note again that Exodus 20:5 states, *"I the LORD thy God am a jealous God."* God desires you and me to worship Him and be in close fellowship with Him. When we walk away from Him, He does not go away and pout, nor does He wipe us from His memory. To the contrary, He goes after us. He does everything He can do to win us back. But He does it in a tough love way.

So often we human beings try to win other people's affection *Don't do this its not Right* by giving them the best we have to offer. The more they hurt us, reject us, scorn us, speak ill of us, or disavow us, the more we try to win them over with lavish praise, coddling behavior, expressions of affection, or expensive gifts. The person who observes such behavior from afar often concludes, "That's sick!" And it is. It's spiritually and emotionally the exact opposite of what needs to be done.

God doesn't punish us outright, but God does leave us to experience the consequences of our disobedience and our turning away. It's as if He says, "You want other gods? You want to worship the gods of your neighbors? Well, then, you'll have to put up with those neighbors. You'll have to take what those neighbors dish out to you."

Is God being mean?

Not at all. He is chastising us and teaching us the consequences of our willful choice to disobey. He is teaching us the great limitations of all other gods. He is teaching us that a life without Him is a life that is unbearable. He is doing the most positive thing that can be done to win us back—and doing it in a way that we come back worshipping Him, respecting Him, honoring Him, and truly loving Him with our entire beings.

Warnings Are to Be Heeded

I once talked to a woman who had been in an automobile accident. Her car was totaled, and so was the car that hit her. It was a miracle that she wasn't injured. I asked her what happened, and she said to me: "I failed to heed a yield sign." Then she went on, "It didn't matter that the sign was behind a large bush—the sign was in effect even if I couldn't see it."

Many people are living like that today. They are failing to yield to the commandments of God. They are moving through their lives as if the commandments of God are of no consequence.

They are wrong. God's commandments are in effect even if people don't know them, believe them, or heed them.

A generation of Israelites rose up that hadn't seen the great works of the Lord, didn't keep the commandments, and didn't love God with single-hearted devotion. They didn't heed!

What did this new generation of Israelites do? God's Word says:

> *And the children of Israel did evil in the sight of the Lord, and served Baalim: and they forsook the Lord God of their fathers, which brought them out of the land of Egypt, and followed other gods, of the gods of the people that were round about them, and bowed themselves unto them, and provoked the Lord to anger. And they forsook the Lord, and served Baal and Ashtaroth. And the anger of the Lord was hot against Israel, and he delivered them into the hands of spoilers that spoiled them, and he sold them into the hands of their enemies round about, so that they could not any longer stand before their enemies. Whithersoever they went out, the hand of the Lord was against them for evil, as the Lord had said, and as the Lord had sworn unto them: and they were greatly distressed.* (Judg. 2:11–15)

The Israelites started worshipping Baal and Ashteroth, and the Lord allowed enemies to come in and "spoil" them.

We have a concept today of spoiling that isn't at all what the writers of the King James Version of the Bible had in mind. To many of us, *to spoil* means to give an abundance of good things to a person. At that time, *to spoil* meant to stain, soil, cause to rot, create a bad reputation, or cause an unhealthy psyche. *To spoil* meant to cause another person to experience pain and discomfort.

God allowed the *"spoilers"* to come and do this to His people.

He allowed the enemies of the Israelites to come into the land and take all the good things away from them, and then force them into servitude so they couldn't even stand up before their enemies. Instead, they had to bow down in slave labor.

The Israelites did not keep God's supreme commandment.

But God kept His word.

He always does.

When the Israelites stopped obeying, they had every good reason to grow faint in their hearts. They had no reason to think God would give them a victory. They had no reason to believe God would prosper them. They had no basis on which to hope for success. They had cut off the supply line of their deliverance. They were living in a state of being convicted and sentenced.

Where are you today in your worship of God only?

Where are you today in keeping His commandments, teaching His commandments to your children, and loving Him with your whole heart, mind, and soul?

Have you fallen into the lure of worshipping false gods?

3

The Lure of Idols and the Worship of False Gods

Idol worship doesn't happen overnight. It is a slow and often seductive process. That was true in the time of the Israelites, and it is true now.

Most of the people who genuinely know the Lord and then turn away from Him do so over time and through a series of decisions they make. They don't go from loving the Lord and worshipping Him with great shouts of praise on Sunday, and end up in the depths of sin on Monday. If that's the case, then in all likelihood, the person didn't genuinely know the Lord in the first place—he or she only knew how to put on an act and sing all the songs and go through the motions of religion.

No, in most cases, the turning to idols is a slow process. It's a predictable process, however. It's a process we can chart.

The First Step: Tolerating False Gods

Let's look at the Israelites. At first, they only tolerated false gods. They took a "live and let live" attitude toward their enemies and the gods of their enemies. They sought to make friends with the people whom God said were their foes. *PAY attentio*

Now, it's one thing to make the acquaintance of people who are sinners if your desire and motivation is to win those people to Christ. You have to know a little about individuals sometimes to know how best to present the Gospel to them. But never in the Bible are we called to become friends with sinners. Sinners drag saints down into sin far more than saints drag sinners down the aisle to accept Christ.

Never are we to seek to make friends with someone whom God calls our enemy or His enemy. God desires to free us, deliver us, rescue us, and protect us from our enemies. Enemies are those who will turn on you in a moment; enemies seek your demise; enemies are out for themselves first and you last. A foe cannot be a friend. *Are you heeding this*

The Israelites didn't obey God when it came to wiping out their enemies. Instead, they sought to coexist with them. They began to tolerate their presence and their gods.

What are you putting up with today? What are you allowing in your home with the excuse that you are just trying to keep peace? To what sin are you exposing yourself at work or in your community, in the name of not making waves, or in the hopes of appearing politically correct or tolerant? *Whats going on?*

An idol is anything that diverts your affection, your time, your resources, your desire, or your allegiance so that when a moment of decision arises, you choose that idol rather than God. If the decision comes up, "Do I spend a little time with something I like and desire, or do I spend a little time with God?" and you choose anything other than God, that thing you choose is an idol. If the question arises, "Do I spend a little money on this experience or thing or person I associate with pleasure, or do I spend a little money on furthering the kingdom of God?" and you choose anything other than God, that item you choose is an idol to you. *Note this*

Idols come in many different forms.

Going to a ball game instead of going to church is a form of idol worship.

"Just having to have" that possession instead of paying your tithe is a form of idol worship.

Spending time with a person to the neglect of your personal life of prayer and devotional reading of God's Word is a form of idol worship.

Idols aren't just things made of wood and stone. They aren't just possessions. They are also relationships, experiences, careers, activities, social obligations, and political alliances.

Jesus said very plainly, *"No man can serve two masters: for either he will hate the one, and love the other; or else he will hold to the one, and despise the other. Ye cannot serve God and mammon"* (Matt. 6:24). He wasn't saying that we can't hold down a job, own things, have friends, or have fun; He was saying that we can't give our allegiance and our loyalty to anything other than God and truly be His followers. We can't serve more than one master—we can't take directives or receive guidance from more than one supreme source.

Jesus said, *"He that loveth father or mother more than me is not worthy of me: and he that loveth son or daughter more than me is not worthy of me. And he that taketh not his cross, and followeth after me, is not worthy of me"* (Matt. 10:37–38). Those are hard words to hear, and hard words to live out, but they are God's truth.

Jesus wasn't saying that we aren't to love our families or seek to have a loving relationship with our parents, spouses, or children. Rather, He was saying that in comparison to our love for Him, there should be no comparison. He was saying that our supreme love belongs to Him and to Him alone. No person has a right to be loved on the same level as God!

Any other person or thing or experience that takes the top spot in our affection and desire, other than Christ Jesus, is an idol.

Let me ask you two tough questions. Do you have an idol in your life? Even if you don't personally have an idol, are you tolerating idols in your home or family?

The Second Step: Incorporating Idols into Your Life

The next step after tolerating idols in the lives of those around you is to make room for them in your own life.

Some of God's best and brightest people started down a wrong path when they began to incorporate idols into their lives. One of King Saul's sons was named Eshbaal. Jonathan, son of Saul, inserted the name "Baal" into the name of one of his sons, Meribbaal. (See 1 Chronicles 8:33–34.)

Solomon, called the wisest man in history, wasn't at all wise when it came to marrying women who were the daughters of potential enemies. He took wives from the Moabites, Ammonites, Edomites, Zidonians, and Hittites, and these wives *"turned away his heart after other gods: and his heart was not perfect with the LORD his God, as was the heart of David his father"* (1 Kings 11:4).

Solomon knew better. He had been taught better. In fact, this same passage that describes Solomon's falling away also says that Solomon loved women *"of the nations concerning which the LORD said unto the children of Israel, Ye shall not go in to them, neither shall they come in unto you: for surely they will turn away your heart after their gods"* (1 Kings 11:2).

The Third Step: Serving Idols

After tolerating idols in the lives of others and then incorporating idols into your own life, comes the final step toward idol worship: serving a false god.

To worship a false god meant to build a shrine to it—perhaps build a statue of it or a temple for it. It meant getting involved in rituals and feasts associated with that false deity. It meant building an altar to the deity—sometimes it even meant planting a grove of trees in the name of a deity. It meant making offerings of food and drink to the false god.

Let me point out to you a very simple but obvious truth throughout the Old Testament: False gods take a great deal of care and feeding.

Many people seem to think that all God's preachers are only out to collect offerings and bring in money for the church; they believe God requires a great deal of their money and time. The fact is, God requires only one-tenth of His people's money, and He says that He will take that tenth we give and pour it back out to us in overflowing abundance. God says He will give back to us to the point that *"there shall not be room enough to receive it"* (Mal. 3:10). Not only that, but God will rebuke all things that seek to devour the giver's life—God will move against the forces of evil that seek to steal from you, cheat you, shortchange you, underpay you, or embezzle your substance. (See Malachi 3:11.) In very plain terms, God promises He will give back to those who give to Him far more than they can ever give!

Giving to God, therefore, becomes the best form of financial investment and security a person can ever have.

People today pour thousands of dollars into the stock market in hopes that some of that money will grow and produce a harvest down the line.

God says, "Give to Me the tenth, and I will multiply it back to you." His promise is one you can count on!

In sharp contrast to the tenth that God requires, false gods want all a person has. They are never satisfied. There's no amount you can give to a false god and come away with any kind of assurance that you have given all that is required. Stop to think about the various idols in the world today that demand time and money...and keep on demanding time and money...and keep on ...and keep on. Stop to think about all the cults you know that require a person sell all and live in a commune that has a pitifully short supply of even life's basic necessities. Stop to think about all the false religions that require a person to sacrifice and sacrifice and sacrifice, with no end in sight.

False gods always deplete the resources of those who serve them—they are evil and evil always seeks to steal, kill, and destroy. (See John 10:10.)

Furthermore, idols never give back like God always gives back.

False gods never provide the thing you were hoping to get from them in the first place. They don't give back fertility or virility or health or life.

False gods don't give the love, the blessing, the satisfaction, the meaning, the fulfillment, or the joy that the idol worshipper is hoping to gain.

False gods are incapable of giving anything eternal.

False gods never go beyond what human beings are capable of doing! Idols have:

- eyes that cannot see
- ears that cannot hear
- lips that cannot speak
- feet that cannot walk

Idols only "see" what their owners want them to see, or surmise that they see. Idols "hear" and "say" only what their owners want them to hear and say. Idols only go where their owners carry them.

To serve a false god brings no benefit beyond a very short-lived emotional response. Any time you base your life on a short-term high of any kind, you are setting yourself up for a long-term low of the worst kind!

An idol that can't genuinely give back anything of value to the idol worshipper certainly cannot give back more than what is given to it. Idols are takers of our substance and value, not givers of blessing.

Jesus said, *"Seek ye first the kingdom of God, and his righteousness; and all these things* [your earthly physical and material needs] *shall be added unto you"* (Matt. 6:33). The genuine stuff of life doesn't come at the foot of an idol; it comes at the foot of the Cross.

Yes, some of God's best and brightest fell into serving false gods. Solomon not only *"turned away his heart after other gods"* but the Bible tells us this:

> For Solomon went after Ashtoreth the goddess of the Zidonians, and after Milcom the abomination of the Ammonites....Then did Solomon build an high place for Chemosh, the abomination of Moab, in the hill that is before Jerusalem, and for Molech, the abomination of the children of Ammon. And likewise did he for all his strange wives, which burnt incense and sacrificed unto their gods.
> (1 Kings 11:5, 7–8)

Solomon built a temple for a false god just a stone's throw from the great Temple in Jerusalem!

God was so angry at Solomon for doing this that He refused to allow his son to take the throne over all Israel. Instead, the heirs of Solomon only took the throne over one tribe, Judah. And God said He allowed that only because He had made a covenant with Solomon's father, David. (See 1 Kings 11:9–13.)

Another king of Israel, Ahab, married a woman from a false religion: Jezebel. She was a daughter of Ethbaal, king of the Zidonians. In fact, Jezebel's name probably should have been spelled

Jezebaal. Her family members were big-time Baal worshippers, and it was only a matter of time before Ahab *"went and served Baal, and worshipped him"* (1 Kings 16:31).

The son of Ahab took Baal worship to an even greater extent—he built temples to Baal in Jerusalem, the holy city of God.

Once a person begins to serve a false god, that service deepens and continues. It can run for generation after generation. It becomes the tradition.

Always take a close look at the things you have just accepted as tradition in your life. Not all traditions are things that should be traditions—and some things that are traditions should never be cast aside!

A Subtle Progression, But Always a Downfall!

The progression to idol worship is often very subtle. A little tolerance turns into a greater amount of tolerance for evil in others around us. A tolerance of evil very subtly turns into dabbling in evil, and eventually, finding ways we can incorporate evil into our lives—perhaps not openly or to a great extent, but a little at a time. The more we incorporate evil into our lives, the more likely we are to incorporate more evil. Once evil is incorporated, it's just one step closer to worshipping or idolizing those things that are against God's commandments.

The progression may be subtle, but the downfall is always a certainty!

Who Are Baal and Ashteroth?

The names Baal and Ashteroth show up throughout the Old Testament. The names first appear in the years after Joshua led the Israelites. The Israelites seemed to focus specifically on these false gods and to worship the idols built to them.

Who are these false gods? Baal was the chief fertility god of the Canaanites. Ashteroth was the female counterpart to Baal. Sexual acts were at the foundation of worship to these two false gods. People worshipped Baal and Ashteroth, in part, through sexual intercourse with the priests and priestesses who were devoted to these deities.

Baal worship existed for many centuries in the greater Middle East. Baal worship was very strong—the desire to worship something and the desire for sexual gratification became mixed up and warped. The desire for the great joy that comes in genuine worship of God and the great emotional release that comes with sex became confused. (Baal worship existed for many centuries in the greater Middle East.)

The Israelites, no doubt, began to like how they felt when they worshipped Baal because they liked the gratification they received in their bodies.

A Very Emotional Form of Worship

The worship of Baal was also filled with intense emotion. Now, I have nothing against emotion as a part of worship. My church is a church of singing and raising hands and dancing in the aisles and shouting for joy! We believe in giving God more emotion than what is given to a professional football game with a tied score and two minutes to go and the ball on the two-yard line!

Emotions, however, are not a substitute for knowing the truth of God's Word. Emotions are the icing on the cake. Emotions allow you to express the truth you know with all your being, including your voice, your hands, and your feet.

Know this—just because a church allows for emotional expression does not automatically mean that church is rooted in truth. You have to take a look at what is being taught, and, even more, at how what is being taught is being lived out in the lives of the people who are part of that church.

In 1 Kings 18 we read about a great contest between Elijah, the prophet of God, and four hundred fifty prophets of Baal and four hundred fifty prophets of the grove (where Ashteroth was served). It was a showdown witnessed by a great many people. Elijah issued the challenge:

> *Let them therefore give us two bullocks; and let them choose one bullock for themselves, and cut it in pieces, and lay it on wood, and put no fire under: and I will dress the other bullock, and lay it on wood, and put no fire under: and call ye on the name of your gods, and I will call on the name of the LORD: and the God that answereth by fire, let him be God. And all the people answered and said, It is well spoken.*
>
> (1 Kings 18:23–24)

Elijah then let the prophets of Baal choose which bullock they wanted to sacrifice. The prophets dressed it and began to call upon Baal to send fire. They called from morning until noon, saying, *"O Baal, hear us. But there was no voice, nor any that answered. And they leaped upon the altar which was made"* (v. 26). At noon, Elijah mocked them and said:

> *Cry aloud: for he is a god; either he is talking, or he is pursuing, or he is in a journey, or peradventure he sleepeth, and must be awaked. And they cried aloud, and cut themselves after their manner with knives and lancets, till the blood gushed out upon them.*   (1 Kings 18:27–28)

Baal worship for these prophets involved shouting, dancing about on an altar, and mutilating themselves with knives and lancets. It was a loud, lewd, emotional, bloody form of worship.

As is virtually always the case, the style of worship of a people reflects how they perceive their god. They saw Baal as a loud, lewd, emotional, bloody god who delighted in the physical sacrifice of the people who sought to worship him.

What Baal required was the one-hundred-percent opposite of what God requires.

The apostle Paul wrote, *"I beseech you therefore, brethren, by the mercies of God, that ye present your bodies a living sacrifice, holy, acceptable unto God, which is your reasonable service"* (Rom. 12:1).

God never requires a person to commit suicide or mutilate his body in any way in order to please Him. Jesus Christ is the only person God ever asked to die. God asks us to present to Him our lives and to serve Him with living, whole, healthy service. Such living is called a sacrifice because we begin to live for God instead of ourselves. Living for self is the norm in our world. Living for God means giving up a worldly perspective and many things in the world, and therefore it is a sacrifice.

Let me make this little aside—any time you hear about a person who commits suicide in an act of terrorism in order to gain the favor of their god, that person is not serving the God of Abraham, Isaac, and Jacob. That person is not serving the God we serve as Christians.

God calls the sacrifice He desires a *"living sacrifice."* It means a sacrifice of our time, our talent, our spiritual gifts, our praise, and our ministry service. He describes this living sacrifice as being *"holy"* and *"acceptable"* and *"reasonable."* Those three words are ones we need to write on our minds with indelible ink.

Holy

A holy sacrifice is one that is dedicated to God and God alone. We are never to give what belongs to God to any other person or organization.

Acceptable

I have never met a mentally healthy person who does not have a pretty good idea about what acceptable behavior is in a civilized society.

The worship of Baal appealed to all of man's lower instincts—man's base nature.

The worship of God always calls us to elevate all of our instincts. We are to think higher thoughts, have higher morals, have higher ethical standards, and have a higher regard for human life.

Most important, the sacrifice we make of our lives is always acceptable to God. He always takes note of it and receives it fully and rewards it. We may not make a perfect sacrifice—after all, only a perfect person can make a perfect sacrifice, which is why the sacrifice of the perfect Jesus resulted in a perfect sacrifice for the sins of all mankind—but we are to make the best and highest sacrifice of ourselves that we can make. When we give to God with a pure motive, a pure heart, and a purity of desire, God accepts our sacrifice and then rewards it. He uses it to work all things together for good to us and to all other believers on the earth. He uses it to win souls and edify the saints.

Reasonable

The worship of the one true and living God is to be performed with a sound mind. A person has to be out of his mind to cut himself with knives and lancets and jump about on an altar to try to get a dead god made of stone to call down fire on a dead animal. In fact, if we saw that happening today, you can be assured that person would be locked up in a mental hospital. One of the saddest facts about false religions is that the people who worship in these unreasonable ways don't recognize that they are being unreasonable. They are mentally deluded.

God calls His people to reason with Him...to be renewed in their minds to understand the deeper truths of god...to reflect and meditate upon and study the Word. All these are behaviors of thinking, rational, reasonable people.

Part of what makes our sacrifice reasonable is that there's a good reason for doing it. A good reason is one that can be proven on this earth.

43

In the twelfth chapter of Romans, the apostle Paul gave very good reasons for presenting ourselves as living sacrifices. He said that such a sacrifice marked by holiness, acceptability, and reason produced an environment in which love and ministry one to another could flourish. It was in the context of our presenting our bodies as living sacrifices that Paul called the early church to become *"one body in Christ, and every one members one of another"* (v. 5). It was in this context that the ministry gifts of prophecy, practical ministry, teaching, exhortation, giving, and acts of mercy were to be performed. It was in this context that people were to show affection for one another, show diligence in conducting their business affairs, and be fervent in their service to the Lord. It was in this context that people were to rejoice in hope, be patient in tribulation, be quick to pray, give to further the Gospel, and show generous hospitality.

The more you seek to give yourself as a living sacrifice to the Lord—pursuing all that is regarded as pure, holy, and righteous to Him—the more you are going to love, the greater you are going to be in your ministry, and the more godly you are going to be in character. You are going to be a walking testimony to God's love, mercy, forgiveness, care, and concern.

All these are reasonable outcomes that can be observed and evaluated reasonably and objectively.

Baal Gave No Answer

The prophets of Baal got no response in their showdown with Elijah. As I stated earlier, no false god is ever able to respond as the worshippers of that false god desire. There was no voice, no fire, no sign of anything from Baal. In fact, there wasn't any action on Mount Carmel until Elijah took over just before the time of the evening sacrifice.

Elijah called the people to come close to him. He repaired the altar of the Lord on that site, which had been broken down. He took twelve stones and rebuilt the altar in the name of the Lord, built a trench of water around it, put wood on the altar and the bullock in pieces, then filled four barrels with water and poured it on the burnt sacrifice and on the wood. He poured four more barrels...and then four more...until the water ran into the trench around the altar. And then at the precise time of the evening sacrifice, Elijah said a very simple two-sentence prayer:

> LORD God of Abraham, Isaac, and of Israel, let it be known this day that thou art God in Israel, and that I am thy servant, and that I have done all these things at thy word. Hear me, O LORD, hear me, that this people may know that thou art the LORD God, and that thou hast turned their heart back again.
> (1 Kings 18:36–37)

And immediately, the fire of the Lord fell! It consumed the burnt sacrifice, the wood, and even the stones and the dust and all the water in the trench. It all vaporized in fire before the eyes of those gathered there.

Now, there was reason for some holy, acceptable, *living* emotion!

The Bible says that when the people saw this, they fell on their faces and said, *"The LORD, he is the God; the LORD, he is the God"* (v. 39). The implication is that they stayed on their faces and kept saying those words of praise over and over until Elijah called an end to the praise service and said, *"Take the prophets of Baal; let not one of them escape"* (v. 40). Elijah then took the prophets to the brook Kishon and there slew them at God's command. (See 1 Kings 18:40.)

Built on the Flesh

Everything associated with the worship of Baal and Ashteroth was fleshly—sexual and emotional. Every aspect of this form of worship was unholy, unacceptable to God, and unreasonable. In serving Baal and Ashteroth, the Israelites shut God out of their lives—they slammed the door on His involvement with them.

So many times I hear people say, "God doesn't care what I do Monday through Saturday as long as I show up at church on Sunday. God doesn't care how I live as long as I declare that Jesus is my Savior."

What dangerous, disastrous, deadly statements!

God cares what you do and how you live every second of every day of your entire life. He cares about what you think, what you take into your life, what you say, what you do, where you go, who you go with, how you look and act and respond. There isn't a detail of your life that God doesn't want to transform into something that fits His picture of purity, righteousness, and holiness. And the reason He cares and wants you to become pure, righteous, and holy is so He might bless you with every blessing He has for you.

Now what do you want?

Do you want Baal and Ashteroth? Or do you want God? *I want*

Do you want the temporary, momentary, fleeting gratification of your flesh? Or do you want the lasting, eternal, satisfying blessing of God? *I want God*

Even before he took on the prophets of Baal and Ashteroth in a challenge, Elijah asked this sobering question of the children of Israel who had gathered on Mount Carmel: *"How long halt ye between two opinions? if the LORD be God, follow him: but if Baal, then follow him"* (1 Kings 18:21).

At the time Elijah asked this question, the people stood in silence. The Bible says, *"The people answered him not a word"* (v. 21).

The fact is, their silence spoke volumes. They weren't sure which one they wanted to follow.

But by the end of the day, they cried out, *"The LORD, he is the God; the LORD, he is the God"* (1 Kings. 18:39).

Who are you following today? The impulses of the flesh and the lure of the devil? Or are you following the guidance of the Holy Spirit, seeking to know everything you can know about the commandments of God the Father and seeking to replicate in your world the life-giving words and deeds of Jesus Christ?

Don't wait until the end of the day—or the end of your life—to decide. You may be too long in deciding. Make a decision now.

My decision is following Jesus who died for me + thank for holy spirit! thank you Papa God for loving me. given me another chance to serve you.

4

Trusting God for Your
Deliverance

I once heard a woman justify her sin this way: "The only thing
that matters to God is that I put Him first. He doesn't care what
I put second, third, or fourth."

She was wrong. The truth is:

When you serve Baal, God bails out.

God doesn't just want to be first in your life. He wants to be
first, last, and only. When God says, "Have no other gods before
Me," He doesn't mean, "Put no other gods in first place." He means,
"Don't let another god be seen in My sight!"

The Israelites brought God's wrath upon themselves through
their disobedience to God's supreme commandment.

But that isn't the end of the story. The silver lining of good
news—life-changing, wonderful news—was this and is this:

*Nevertheless the LORD raised up judges, which delivered
them out of the hand of those that spoiled them.*

(Judg. 2:16)

48

Let me assure you today, no matter what you're facing, and no matter whether you are intentionally or unintentionally the cause of your own fate, God has a "nevertheless" opportunity for you!

Then God raised up judges.

Then God raised up judges.

Then God raised up judges.

Let those words sink deep into your soul today. God is raising up a judge! God is making a way! God is about to reveal a plan! God is standing ready, just waiting for you to call upon Him so He can start your deliverance!

Oh, what good news that is!

But we can't get to the glory part of this move on God's part too soon. Read what God's Word says about how the Israelites responded to the judges God raised up:

> *And yet they* [the Israelites] *would not hearken unto their judges, but they went a whoring after other gods, and bowed themselves unto them: they turned quickly out of the way which their fathers walked in, obeying the commandments of the LORD; but they did not so. And when the LORD raised them up judges, then the LORD was with the judge, and delivered them out of the hand of their enemies all the days of the judge: for it repented the LORD because of their groanings by reason of them that oppressed them and vexed them. And it came to pass, when the judge was dead, that they returned, and corrupted themselves more than their fathers, in following other gods to serve them, and to bow down unto them; they ceased not from their own doings, nor from their stubborn way.* (Judg. 2:17–19)

The overall pattern was not a good one!

Before we explore how God raised up judges for deliverance, we should explore exactly who those judges were and what they were called and authorized to do.

Who Were the "Judges"?

The word we translate as *"judges"* is the Hebrew word *shoptim*. To be a *shopet,* or a judge, meant something far different back then than what it means in our world today. Judges today are involved in our legal system—they preside over our courts of law. The Hebrew word for judge had nothing to do with the law. It was used to describe someone who had authority over the people.

An Old Testament judge, for all practical purposes, was the head of state, although he was not technically a king. In essence, he was the leader of the legislative branch, the executive branch, and the judicial system all rolled into one. He exercised authority, under God, in both military and civil matters, but he had no court, no taxation system, no palace, and no legislative system for developing or enacting laws.

Throughout the history of Israel, God was considered to be the Supreme Judge. In Judges 11:27, God is called *hashshopet* in Hebrew. He was the "Judge" with a capital J!

The judges always reported directly to God—not to a king, a priest, or any other leader. They were raised up by God, appointed by God, and directed by God.

For Specific Times and Situations

God's judgments were part of the instruction that God gave to His people, along with the commandments. His judgments were essentially the rulings about how His people were to keep the commandments and in what manner they were to live in peace in the land He had set apart for them. Judgments tended to be timely and related to circumstances and situations. The commandments of God, in contrast, are eternal and absolute; they do not vary from one person to the next, one generation to the next, one culture to the next, one race to the next, one gender to the next, or one situation to the next. Even though judgments were more timely, they also reflected absolute principles.

No Heirs to Assume the Role of Judge

Although kings, and even the priests in Israelite history, had heirs who took their place in leadership, none of the judges was followed by a rightful, God-authorized heir. Each of them was raised up by God for a specific generation.

The reason they were raised up can be summed up in one word—deliverance. The judges were the God-appointed deliverers of the people of Israel.

The Specific Need For Deliverance

The judges appeared in the history of the Israelites for only about two hundred years—after Joshua and before King Saul. (This was fourteen hundred to twelve hundred years before Jesus.)

Let me recap very quickly for you the state of things for the Israelites at that time.

Abraham, Isaac, and Jacob (also called Israel) had lived in this area called the Promised Land. They had co-existed with the Canaanites and other pagan peoples, roaming the area with their flocks and herds but not truly ruling any one area. Then, in response to a great drought in the land, the children of Jacob had gone down into Egypt. There, they were given land and provision from one of Jacob's sons, Joseph, whom God had raised up into the position of being second in command to Pharaoh. The children of Israel settled in the area called Goshen, and they remained in this territory of Egypt for four hundred years.

The children of Israel eventually became slaves to the Egyptians, and they remained slaves until their miraculous departure from Egypt under the leadership of Moses.

Moses had been commanded by God to lead the Israelites out of Egypt and *"to bring them up out of that land unto a good land and a large, unto a land flowing with milk and honey; unto the place of the Canaanites, and the Hittites, and the Amorites, and the Perizzites, and the Hivites, and the Jebusites"* (Exod. 3:8).

Pharaoh and the Egyptians experienced great plagues sent by God and eventually, in the aftermath of the death angel that killed all the firstborn in Egypt, let God's people go. God miraculously parted the Red Sea so they could walk across on dry land. The Israelites finally were headed for the land God had promised to them!

Because of their disobedience, however, in failing to trust God to give them the land He had promised, the Israelites wandered in the wilderness between Egypt and the Promised Land for forty years. This was a time when God gave them His commandments for moral and ethical excellence, provided for them in miraculous ways, and, most importantly, set up the system of worship they were to follow. It was a time of great hardship, and literal sacrifice, as the Israelites learned how to obey God. There were few rewards and no luxuries.

After forty years, God sovereignly parted the waters of the Jordan River—just as He had sovereignly parted the waters of the Red Sea—and God's people moved from the wilderness into the Promised Land.

In a relatively short period of time, the Israelites had defeated major strongholds in Canaan. They were propelled to victory again and again because of Joshua's leadership in listening to God's battle plans and Joshua's great trust in God's power to keep the promises He had made to His people.

At the time of the judges, the Israelites had been in Canaan for about a generation and a half—the latter years of Joshua's life plus a full generation after Joshua's death.

Let me also tell you what was going on in the greater region at the time of the judges. First, iron had just been discovered, and this strong metal was being used in both agriculture and warfare.

The enemies of the Israelites, almost overnight, had a very new and powerful tool with which to fight against God's people. The technology of the times was stacked against the Israelites.

Second, Canaan—the Promised Land to the Israelites—was traditionally an area of tremendous ongoing conflict. The area we know as Israel today was a bridge of land between Egypt to the south and west, and the two great empires that emerged to the north and northeast—the Assyrian Empire and the Babylonian Empire. The area of Canaan was always caught in the middle like the rope between two bullies engaged in a tug-of-war fight.

If you look at a map today, Egypt is still Egypt. The heart of Assyria is the nation of Syria today. The heart of Babylonia is Iraq and part of Iran today. You don't need me to tell you that these giant nations in the greater Middle East are still struggling to gain supremacy!

Through the centuries, Egypt would periodically move north, push back Assyria or Babylonia, and gain control over the trade-route wealth of the area. Then Assyria or Babylonia would rise up and push south, and Egypt would withdraw back across the Nile River. The area in between was nearly always under invasion or fear of an invasion from one great superpower or another.

At this particular time of two hundred years—which we think of as a very long time, but in the history of that part of the world, it's very brief—the leaders of Egypt, Assyria, and Babylonia were all fairly well occupied with political problems in their own nations. This left a little vacuum in which much lesser powers tried to move in and drive out the Israelites. The Philistines pushed in from the Mediterranean Coast, the area we know as the Gaza Strip today. The Midianites attacked from the eastern deserts, and so forth. Again and again, the Israelites found themselves suffering from great persecution and war waged against them.

But it wasn't the military or political strength of the Israelites' enemies that was at the heart of the need for the judges. As I stated in the previous chapter, the real need for the judges was spiritual.

Spiritual Types and Shadows

One of the most amazing facts about the Bible is that it conveys truth to us on a variety of levels, some of which we aren't able to grasp until we personally reach a certain level of spiritual maturity. A person never outgrows his or her need to read the Bible; there's always eternal truth to be gleaned from its pages, and that truth is not only eternal, but also timely and applicable directly to the reader's life. It's always amazing to me that every time I open the Bible to read it in-depth or study a particular portion of it, the Bible seems to speak directly to me. It's as if God said, "Write down these words because G. E. Patterson is going to need them a few thousand years from now!"

Another amazing thing happens. When I revisit a passage after a couple of years or even several months, I am amazed to find that I learn something new from the passage, even though I previously had studied it in great detail. It's as if God embedded new nuggets of gold into the old mine just so I would find them on my next reading! I find myself saying again and again as I read the Bible, "Why didn't I see that before?" In some cases, I wasn't ready, perhaps, to see the truth God wanted to reveal to me. In some cases, I could see that this new truth was exactly what I needed for a particular situation I was facing. In other cases, I could see that I needed to learn some other things from God's Word so I would be able to connect a particular passage to other portions of the Scripture and see a deeper, more expansive truth.

God's Word is always eternal. Always!

God's Word is always timely—right for today. Always!

That's one of the ways we know it is God's Word—it bears His nature. He is always and forever the same. He is always revealing a new aspect of Himself to us.

God is always and forever the sovereign King of the universe, the Creator, Sustainer, and Ruler of all things at every moment in the too-long-to-calculate expanse of eternity.

God is also closer to us than the breath of our bodies. He knows every intimate detail of our lives, including our deepest, innermost thoughts and desires that we sometimes don't even know ourselves.

When we read God's Word, therefore, we can glean truth at various levels. There's always the surface reality of what is happening historically in the lives of God's people. But there's another reality that has to do with symbols—various objects in the tangible world that represent various principles or entities in the supernatural realm. There's also the reality that has to do with what a story means in terms of character development, obedience, or ways to apply God's principles to our everyday lives.

Then there's the reality that we call "types and shadows." Sometimes a person or a group of people reflects a process. The actions of a person reveal how God works in the lives of His people—the principles, methods, circumstances, and outcomes that occur when people act a certain way or adopt certain beliefs. More specifically, a person in the Old Testament may be a foreshadow of Jesus or the work of the Holy Spirit in the lives of Christians today. A situation in the natural, material realm may be a type of a broader spiritual situation.

That's what I believe we have in the book of Judges. There's a reason for us to read and study this book about the people and events of more than three thousand years ago because the spiritual processes and the work of God written in it are highly applicable to our lives today.

The Conditions for Possessing the Land Were Spiritual

Not only was it a spiritual need—actually, a spiritual depravity—that put the Israelites in a position where they needed deliverance, but the process God set out for their deliverance was also primarily a spiritual process.

Let me remind you that God swore to give the land to the Israelites. (See Deuteronomy 6:10.) You can be assured that if God swears to give you anything, you will receive it! God's promises are sure. They always come to pass.

Now, some of God's promises have conditions attached to them—if you do this, God will do that. Other promises are not conditional.

God's promise to give the Israelites the Promised Land was not conditional. The Israelites, however, did have a responsibility when it came to keeping the land—of occupying it fully and living in peace from their enemies. The condition that God put in place was this:

> *Thou shalt fear the LORD thy God, and serve him, and shalt swear by his name. Ye shall not go after other gods, of the gods of the people which are round about you; (for the LORD thy God is a jealous God among you) lest the anger of the LORD thy God be kindled against thee, and destroy thee from off the face of the earth. Ye shall not tempt the LORD your God, as ye tempted him in Massah. Ye shall diligently keep the commandments of the LORD your God, and his testimonies, and his statutes, which he hath commanded thee. And thou shalt do that which is right and good in the sight of the LORD: that it may be well with thee, and that thou mayest go in and possess the good land which the LORD sware unto thy fathers, to cast out all thine enemies from before thee, as the LORD hath spoken.* (Deut. 6:13–19)

Those seven verses in the book of Deuteronomy spell out the conditions under which the Israelites were to occupy the land and live in freedom from their enemies. God swore to give them the land, but there were conditions placed on their possessing what God was giving.

The same is true for us today. God promises to give those who believe in Jesus Christ two things: abundant life and eternal life. But there are conditions placed upon us for receiving all the blessings and living in all the fullness of God's promises. Those conditions are the same as those placed upon the Israelites:

- Fear the Lord—which means to revere Him with great awe and respect.

- Serve the Lord—which means to obey all His commandments.

- Worship the Lord only—which means to keep from turning to any other gods.

Important

You can be saved by the shed blood of Jesus and be filled with God's Holy Spirit and still not live fully and freely in the fullness of all God has for you. Your living fully and freely in His fullness depends on your fearing the Lord, serving the Lord, and worshipping the Lord with your whole spirit, mind, and soul.

In speaking to the Israelites, God was speaking to former slaves of Pharaoh. These people had been oppressed and downtrodden and forced into hard labor that broke both their bodies and their spirits. They had been serving Pharaoh. Now God said to them, "Serve Me."

Service to God was not an oppression—it was a their redemption and exaltation as a people!

Service to God was not something that put them down or forced them under—it was the key to their receiving an abundance they had never known before!

Service to God did not break their bodies and spirits—it was the secret to their receiving health and wholeness and spiritual refreshment!

Each of us who call ourselves Christians is a former slave to sin, but sometimes we forget all that slavery to sin involved. Sin binds, shackles, holds back, destroys, diminishes, and results in everlasting death. God calls us to serve Him, but the end result of our service to the Lord is the exact opposite of slavery to sin—in Christ Jesus is freedom, potential, hope, multiplied blessings, and eternal life.

God declared to the Israelites that they were a chosen people—a *"holy people,"* a *"special people,"* a people *"above all people that are upon the face of the earth"* (Deut. 7:6). God chose to love His people and be merciful to them. Moses reminded the Israelites:

> *Know therefore that the Lord thy God, he is God, the faithful God, which keepeth covenant and mercy with them that love him and keep his commandments to a thousand generations; and repayeth them that hate him to their face, to destroy them.* (Deut. 7:9–10)

We are never in a position of negotiating blessings with God.

His rules regarding His blessings and promises are as sure as His commandments and judgments. God says that He will keep covenant and show mercy to those who love Him and keep His commandments. He will have no mercy to those who don't.

Moses said that those who hearken to his *"judgments, and keep, and do them"* are those *"he will love...and bless...and multiply"* (Deut. 7:12–13). It couldn't be more clear.

Battles—Both Natural and Spiritual

Where does this lead us?

It all leads us to the fact that every battle in which Israel fought was not just a historical event, but a deeply spiritual experience. The battles that the Lord authorized and directed and led the Israelites to fight were not human-only events. They were spiritual events. The Lord fought against His enemies, and ultimately against the enemy that was seeking to destroy the souls of His people. God took on the role of the leader of their army. Jehovah-Sabaoth means just that—the Lord God, Captain of the Army.

God's primary concern was not that the people be freed from those who tried to take their farms or their businesses—His concern was that the people be set free from the forces of evil that were trying to dominate their lives and bring about their destruction. He was concerned that the enemy might steal, kill, and destroy His people from the inside out. That's why He moved against the enemies of the Israelites when they cried out to Him.

Notice, too, that at no time did God say, "All right, you've cried out to Me. Now I'm going to let your enemy rule over you for a little bit longer so you'll really appreciate My deliverance of you." That didn't happen. God allowed enemies to gain power over the Israelites because that was the consequence for their doing what was evil in His sight, but once the people had confessed their sin and turned to Him, He always sent a deliverer to free them from bondage. *Thank you Papa God*

God never desires for His people to remain in spiritual bondage. His desire is that we cry out in confession of our sins and repentance in our hearts. And the moment we do, He sets in motion our spiritual deliverance—which leads to our deliverance in the natural.

Four Great Parallels of Truth

Now, before we go any further, let me draw four great parallels of truth for you on the basis of what I've shared thus far.

From Egypt to the Land of Promise

First, in countless ways, the deliverance of the Israelites from Egypt and their crossing over into the Promised Land is like our experience today of being saved and filled with God's Holy Spirit.

God sent His only begotten Son, Jesus Christ, to this earth to declare the truth of God and perform signs and wonders that effectively defeated the enemy of our souls, just as Moses declared the truth of God and performed signs and wonders that caused Pharaoh to eventually "let God's people go." (See John 3:16.)

God's Word tells us that when we believe in Christ Jesus, we go from a path that leads to eternal spiritual death to a path that leads to everlasting spiritual life.

We embark on a journey that takes us from the slavery of sin—and all that the devil would try to do to steal from us, destroy us, and kill us—to an abundant life in which all God's promises of blessing are made available to us. (See John 10:10.)

We go from being fragmented individuals with no real spiritual identity and no restraints upon our fleshly desires, to being a people with an identity as joint heirs with Christ Jesus and the restraints of God's commandments that lead us to lives of purity, holiness, righteousness, and wisdom.

We go from being a people with no eternal home to a people bound for the eternal glory of heaven.

We go from being in bondage to being set free to love and serve the Lord.

And all of that in the hour of our accepting Jesus Christ as our Savior!

In the aftermath of our salvation, most of us went through the waters of baptism, just as the children of Israel crossed through the rolled-back waters of the Red Sea. We emerged cleansed and delivered from the stranglehold and slavery of sin.

60

Wandering in a Wilderness

God begins a process of renewal and spiritual development in every person at the moment of his or her salvation. Unfortunately, countless Christians never go beyond that point. They do not actively and intentionally receive the Holy Spirit into their lives, even though His presence is promised to all who believe in Christ Jesus.

For those who live without the fullness of the Holy Spirit, the Christian life can be hard work. It can be one struggle of faith after another, a continual search for refreshment in the Lord. The Christian life apart from the Holy Spirit is very often a life of legalism and sacrifice—those who don't have an awareness of the Holy Spirit within tend to be people who get caught up in good works. They see God's commands and call to ministry as "have to" obligations. In contrast, those who have the Holy Spirit more often see God's commands and call to ministry as "get to" privileges.

Crossing into God's Land of Promise

The crossing over of the Israelites into the Land of Promise can be likened to what happens when a person is baptized in the Holy Spirit. After all, the Holy Spirit is the promise of God to us. Jesus said to His followers right before His ascension back into heaven, *"Behold, I send the promise of my Father upon you: but tarry ye in the city of Jerusalem, until ye be endued with power from on high"* (Luke 24:49). Jesus was speaking of the Holy Spirit.

With the Holy Spirit comes a crossing over into the full provision, protection, promises, and presence of God. That's the spiritual reality for us of what happened to the Israelites. In the wilderness, the Israelites knew God's provision, protection, promises, and presence, but once they crossed over into Canaan, all those things became theirs with a greater joy and permanence. They were finally in their land. They could finally be who God had called them to be.

Before crossing over the Jordan into Canaan, the Israelites wandered. In the Land of Promise, they settled. The same thing happens to us. Some things are finally decided within us in a definitive, no-turning-back way when we receive the fullness of the Holy Spirit. As the Bible says, we are sealed by the Holy Spirit in Christ forever. The apostle Paul wrote to the Ephesians, *"We should be to the praise of his glory, who first trusted in Christ. In whom ye also trusted, after that ye heard the word of truth, the gospel of your salvation: in whom also after that ye believed, ye were sealed with that holy Spirit of promise"* (Eph. 1:12–13).

The life we live as Holy Spirit-filled and sanctified believers is a life that is the beginning of the wholeness and blessings that are ours on into eternity. The apostle Paul called it the *"earnest of our inheritance"* until we are with the Lord in heaven (Eph. 1:14).

With the Holy Spirit in us, we have full access to all the blessings of God. They are ours, if we will only believe for them, claim them with our faith, move into them as the Holy Spirit leads and guides us, and then use those blessings to bless others. The Holy Spirit makes available to us the "riches of Christ Jesus in glory" (see Phil. 4:19).

"But," you may be saying, "I've been filled with God's Spirit for years, and I'm not living in the fullness of God's provision, protection, promises, and presence. In fact, at times it seems I'm struggling just to keep my head above water, struggling against the devil, struggling to believe, struggling to *feel* God at work in me."

Why is this so? The reasons you are not living out the fullness of a promised-blessed life are likely the same reasons the Israelites did not live in the fullness of the Promised Land that God had ordained for them. Those reasons are the reasons that led to the Israelites needing judges. But before we go down that path, let me share several more parallels of truth with you.

Pay attention page 63

God Is Supreme Judge

The second great truth you must never lose sight of is this: God is your Supreme Judge. Just as He was for the Israelites, He is the Judge with a capital J! He is our Deliverer!

We call the pinnacle of our legal system the Supreme Court. A group of men and women called Supreme Court Justices hand down rulings from that court to effect justice in our land. Let me assure you, God is really your highest Supreme Court Justice. He is the only Judge on the throne of His Supreme Court in Heaven.

What God says goes.

What God declares to be just is justice.

What God commands is the way we must live.

And what God decides in our favor is decided, no matter what the devil may throw at us, do to us, or whisper in our ears.

God is your *my* ultimate Savior, Deliverer, Healer, Restorer, Provider, the Author and Finisher of Your Faith, and the Source of All Blessings. There is no person—no pastor, bishop, evangelist, prophet, or any other servant of God—who can do for you what God can do for you. God uses men and women in appointed ministry callings to be vessels of His power, but Jesus alone is Lord. *Hallelujah*

We often speak of people believing in Jesus as their Savior and Lord. The truth is, we believe in Jesus and accept Him as our Savior, and then we trust in Jesus and follow Him as our Lord. Accepting Jesus as Savior is a process of opening up our lives to allow the Spirit of God to cleanse us and change our nature—from the old sinful man to a new creature that desires to worship God in all ways, in all relationships, in all situations, at all times. (See 2 Corinthians 5:17.) *Let me do your will only youre will.*

In contrast, following Jesus as Lord is a daily, active process of obedience. We don't just casually follow Jesus if He is our Lord. Rather, we seek God's face every morning, asking the Lord, "What do You want me to do today? Where do You want me to go? To

Every morning talk to Jesus, Papa God, Holy Spirit

whom do You want me to speak? What do You want me to say?"
And then, as the Holy Spirit gives us His guidance, we do what He
tells us to do and say. We are one-hundred-percent submitted, or
yielded, to doing God's will when we follow Jesus as Lord.

You can believe in God—but that's not the same as believing
in Christ as your personal Savior. In the same vein, believing in
Christ as your Savior is not the same as following Jesus as your
Lord.

It is when we look to God as our Supreme Judge—the Lord
of our lives—that He wins for us the definitive victories that result
in our laying full claim to all His promises. If there's only one truth
you carry away with you from this book, make it that one. Let me
repeat:

**It is when we look to God as our Supreme
Judge—the Lord of our lives—that He wins for
us the definitive victories that result in our
laying full claim to all His promises.**

That's the message of this entire book in just one sentence!

If you are looking to any person, organization, or entity other
than God to bring you to total victory, success, wholeness, prosperity, and provision—whatever name you want to give to a life that
is balanced, healthy, spiritually strong, and victorious over all life's
problems—you are going to experience failure every time.

God's commandments are to be the laws by which you live.

God's judgments are to be the goals that you aim to imple-
ment and accomplish in your life.

God's principles are the guidelines by which you are to make
specific decisions and solve specific problems.

Your Specific Needs and Challenges

Every generation of Israelites, it seems, faced a specific enemy;
the needs they experienced were very real, and in most cases,

dire. And God didn't choose to deliver them in precisely the same way twice.

God knows you inside out and as someone once said, "He also knows you upside down!" He knows who He created you to be and the purpose for which He designed your life, and He knows all the ways in which you have failed to become that person or live out that purpose.

God dealt with specific enemies with specific judges in specific ways. The same principle holds true for you. God knows precisely what you need. He knows how to deliver you from the enemies that are destroying your peace and bring you to a place of fulfillment, purpose, and joy.

Don't expect God to act on your behalf exactly as He has acted in the life of someone you know, someone you heard about, or someone you'd like to know. He'll follow His absolute commands and His timeless spiritual principles—which is what we will study more closely in this book—but the specifics of His work in your life are designed to address your uniqueness. He works with your personality, your talents, and your skills. He works in your life—in your home, your job, your community, and your church. He works in the context of the history of your life from birth to the present day.

And the good news is this—God can take all the stray threads of your life and weave them into something beautiful. He can work *"all things"* to your eternal good (Rom. 8:28). The fabric He ends up with—called "you"—is going to be a one-of-a-kind tapestry, a genuine work of divine art that has never been created before and will never be seen again.

That's the third great parallel truth we can draw: God's deliverance is for you—all of you!

Don't expect your deliverance to come from your good heritage, your fine genes, your great upbringing, or your family's good name and reputation in your community.

Don't expect your deliverance to come from your children's accomplishments or success.

God's deliverance is for you in your time—which is now!

There's a Struggle for Your Witness

The fourth great parallel we can draw is this: There's a spiritual battle going on that relates directly to you and to your ability to give glory to God.

When you were a sinner—living in the "land of Egypt"—there was a mighty battle in the heavenly realm for your eternal spirit. God wanted to save you and give you eternal life; the devil wanted to keep you in bondage and see you end up in an eternal state of death. God wooed you to Himself. The devil threw every temptation in the book at you to keep you from hearing or heeding God's love song sung in your ear.

When you accepted Jesus as your Savior, the devil lost that battle. God won the struggle for your soul. The angels sang as God forgave your past, removed all guilt and shame from you, and cleansed your heart from *"all unrighteousness"* (1 John 1:9).

From that moment until now, however, the devil has continued to fight against any degree of effective witness you might have. He has sought to bring you to discouragement and despair. He has sought to oppress you to the point where you no longer have any desire or ability to tell others the Good News that Jesus is Savior and Lord. The battle is no longer for your soul—it is for your witness.

Jesus called the devil a *"thief"* and said of him, *"The thief cometh not, but for to steal, and to kill, and to destroy: I am come that they might have life, and that they might have it more abundantly"* (John 10:10).

Look closely at what Jesus said about the enemy that comes at you. The Israelites faced the big three: Egypt, Assyria, and

Babylonia. You face the big three assaults of the devil: theft, death, and irreparable damage.

The devil is at work at all times to steal from you every good thing that God sends your way. He wants others to take a look at you and conclude, "Being a Christian isn't all that great—just look at the poverty, sickness, and shattered life of that person who calls himself a Christian. Just look at the troubles that always seem to dog that so-called saint." The devil wants to steal any witness he can that might cause others to declare, "Jesus is the Lord over all I need."

The devil is at work at all times to kill you, and primarily to kill you on the inside. He wants to kill any semblance of joy, peace, love, faith, patience, or goodness inside you. He desires to stop the flow of God's love into your life, and, further, he desires to assassinate your character! (See Galatians 5:22–23.) He wants others to take a look at you and shake their heads and say, "Just look at the sour expression and slumped shoulders of that woman who says she believes in Jesus. If that's what it feels like on the inside to believe in Jesus, I don't want anything to do with it." The devil wants to steal any witness he can that might possibly cause others to declare, "Jesus is the One who gives me peace deep in my soul, a smile on my face, a confidence in my heart, and a spring to my step."

The devil is at work at all times to destroy you. He doesn't want you to have any reputation of note, any integrity, any ability to function, any authority. He'll do his utmost to keep you from getting the education to turn your talents into usable skills, the money you need to pay your bills, the property you should have to establish your home, the job you can do with excellence or the business you should build, the ministry you are called to have within the body of Christ, or the position of leadership He desires for you to have so you can lift up the name of Jesus in your community. The devil wants others to look at you and say, "There's a broken-down loser."

Here Comes the Judge

He wants to steal any witness you might have that Jesus is your Strength, your Strong Tower, your Defender, your Shield, and the Victor of your life.

Don't let it happen!

Trust God to be your Deliverer!

Choose today to move into the fullness and freedom that God has for you.

I choose today to move into the fulness & freedom that my Papa God has for me in Jesus name who I declare in my Savior & the holy spirit dwelles in me. J. love you lord

Time 7 27 pm Wed. march 6-2024

This morning the holy spirit reminding me of the song I saw the shadow of Christ — I touch the hem of Christ I was healed (feel better) spiritually this morning About 4:00 am 5 or so I got to dance praise & claimed my spiritual healing — Thank you for ...

Thursday 3-7-24

5

Leading the Way with Praise— "Even" Your Praise!

nce, a woman was overheard saying as she purchased her lottery tickets, "O Lord, deliver me." She kept repeating those words as she walked out of the store with a fistful of tickets.

She probably isn't the first, or last, person to trust God to use a lottery or a sweepstakes or a horse race to "deliver" her.

Other people trust a government grant...or a particular leader...or a member of the family...or a favorite preacher...or a new law...or a job opportunity...or the move to a new city to be their agent of deliverance.

The method of deliverance that God has for you may not be at all what you expect. And it may not involve the person or people you had expected to show up.

In these next three chapters, I want to tell you about the first three judges God raised up to deliver His people.

If I asked you right now to name these men for me—with no peeking ahead and no looking at your Bible—I doubt if you could do so. These men are not ones we hear about with great frequency. In all my years as I was growing up, I don't recall hearing a single sermon about them. Nonetheless, they were powerful deliverers used by God in their time.

As we go through their stories, I encourage you to take special note that these men were from different tribes, faced different enemies, and used different methods. Keep in mind also that the principles they display are directly related to the way God brings deliverance into your life:

- God can use anyone for His purposes.

- God can use any method He desires—including all methods known to us and some that are entirely unknown to us.

- With God's anointing power, God's person can do all things.

Othniel Took on an Empire

The first judge God raised up was Othniel, the son of Kenax, who happened to be Caleb's younger brother. Caleb is the man who had stood in faith with Joshua and gave a positive report after spying in Canaan. He and Joshua were the only two of the original Israelites who left Egypt as adults who were allowed to enter the Land of Promise. (See Numbers 14:29–38.)

At the time the Israelites crossed over the Jordan, Caleb was an old man. On his eighty-fifth birthday he said to Joshua,

I am as strong this day as I was in the day that Moses sent me: as my strength was then, even so is my strength now, for war, both to go out, and to come in. Now therefore give me this mountain, whereof the LORD spake in that day; for thou heardest in that day how the Anakims were there, and that

Judah- means Praise

Leading the Way with Praise—"Even" Your Praise!

the cities were great and fenced: if so be the Lord will be with me, then I shall be able to drive them out, as the Lord said.
(Josh. 14:11–12)

What an amazing request this was! Caleb, for his eighty-fifth birthday present, asked Joshua to give him the privilege of conquering the toughest part of Canaan. It was the area where the giants lived. It had a city with a great wall around it. "Give me this place," Caleb said.

What an amazing faith Caleb had! He said, "I can do all things if God is with me. I believe He is with me, so I'll be able to drive out these giants just as God said."

Joshua blessed Caleb and said, "It's yours." Caleb fought the fight and won the territory. This part of Judah, which had Hebron at its center, became Caleb's.

Now I want you to know a very important fact about Caleb—he was from the tribe of Judah. He represented the tribe of Judah at the time the twelve spies were chosen. (See Numbers 13:6.) The name *Judah* literally means praise. When Leah, Judah's mother, gave birth to him, the Bible says she made this declaration: *"Now will I praise the Lord: therefore she called his name Judah"* (Gen. 29:35). Not only did this baby's name mean praise, but his mother was praising the Lord as she gave birth to him.

Again and again in the Scriptures, you are going to find that God sent out the tribe of Judah to lead in conquest. The tribe of Judah was the one tribe that remained intact for rulership by a member of the house of David after Solomon's sin.

It is the tribe of Judah that is first mentioned as fighting against the Canaanites after the death of Joshua. In fact, the book of Judges opens with these verses:

Now after the death of Joshua it came to pass, that the children of Israel asked the Lord, saying, Who shall go up for us against the Canaanites first, to fight against them? And

the LORD said, Judah shall go up: behold, I have delivered the
land into his hand. (Judg. 1:1–2)

And that's exactly what happened. Judah led the way, and the Canaanites and the Perizzites were defeated.

The tribes of Judah and Simeon continued the battle campaign to conquer the territory from the city of Jerusalem south to the city of Hebron. Then they went west and defeated the occupants of Gaza, including the cities of Askelon and Ekron. (Even though Judah and Simeon defeated Jerusalem, the tribe of Benjamin did not drive out the Jebusites who lived in that city, but chose to dwell beside them—which turned out to be a major mistake.)

Judah led the way in securing the Promised Land in the south.

It is also interesting to note that the tribe of Judah received this prophetic blessing from Jacob almost five hundred years prior to their entering the Promised Land:

Judah, thou art he whom thy brethren shall praise: thy hand
shall be in the neck of thine enemies; thy father's children
shall bow down before thee. Judah is a lion's whelp: from
the prey, my son, thou art gone up: he stooped down, he
couched as a lion, and as an old lion; who shall rouse him
up? The sceptre shall not depart from Judah, nor a lawgiver
from between his feet, until Shiloh come; and unto him shall
the gathering of the people be. (Gen. 49:8–10)

Judah went up first. And the spiritual meaning we can draw from that fact is this: Praise is to go up first.

Judah is the first and foremost tribe of praise, deliverance, and leadership. Jesus was from the tribe of Judah and in Him is the fullness of that tribe. All praise is due Him. He is the Deliverer. He is the King of all kings!

All of us have to fight "Canaanites" at some point in our lives. How do we begin that fight? With praise to Jesus, who is worthy of all our praise.

Deliverance through Praise

Let me remind you of one story in the Bible in which God led His people to deliverance through praise. The story is found in 2 Chronicles 20.

Jehoshaphat was king of Judah. He was a powerful influence for good. The Bible tells us that the Lord was with Jehoshaphat *"because he walked in the first ways of his father David, and sought not unto Baalim"* (2 Chron. 17:3). He served the Lord, not Baal. He walked in the commandments of God, and he destroyed the places of worship that had been built to serve false gods. He set up a system for the Levites to teach the Book of the Law throughout all the cities. The Bible says, *"The fear of the LORD fell upon all the kingdoms of the lands that were round about Judah"* (v. 10). When enemies made war against him, his armies defeated them. The land became known for great trade and prosperity. Jehoshaphat personally had *"riches and honour in abundance"* (2 Chron. 18:1).

And then came a major assault. The Moabites, Ammonites, and the people who dwelt in Mount Seir launched a three-pronged attack against Jerusalem.

Jehoshaphat did exactly the right thing. He went to the Lord with humility and a repentant heart. He proclaimed a fast throughout the land, calling upon all the Israelites to come before the Lord in humble repentance. Jehoshaphat took the lead in praying on behalf of the people, stating his total reliance upon the Lord for a victory. He closed his prayer by saying, *"O our God, wilt thou not judge them? for we have no might against this great company that cometh against us; neither know we what to do: but our eyes are upon thee"* (2 Chron. 20:12).

God sent a wonderful message back to Jehoshaphat and the Israelites through a prophetic utterance given to Jahaziel. Note that Jahaziel wasn't the king. But he was somebody the Lord could speak through. That's the kind of person God is looking

73

for today—somebody who will submit to Him, yield everything to Him, and be a willing vessel for any purpose the Lord chooses! Jahaziel said:

> *Hearken ye, all Judah, and ye inhabitants of Jerusalem, and thou king Jehoshaphat, Thus saith the LORD unto you, Be not afraid nor dismayed by reason of this great multitude; for the battle is not yours, but God's. To morrow go ye down against them: behold, they come up by the cliff of Ziz; and ye shall find them at the end of the brook, before the wilderness of Jeruel. Ye shall not need to fight in this battle: set yourselves, stand ye still, and see the salvation of the LORD with you, O Judah and Jerusalem: fear not, nor be dismayed; to morrow go out against them: for the LORD will be with you.*
>
> (2 Chron. 20:15–17)

God told the Israelites exactly when to go. He told them where to find the enemy. He told them to have courage and fear not. And He told them they wouldn't need to fight, but they would need to *"go out against them."*

The next morning, the people rose early to do just as God said. Jehoshaphat gave them these words: *"Hear me, O Judah, and ye inhabitants of Jerusalem; Believe in the LORD your God, so shall ye be established; believe his prophets, so shall ye prosper"* (2 Chron. 20:20).

Faith is put into motion to overcome fear!

And then Jehoshaphat *"appointed singers unto the LORD, and that should praise the beauty of holiness, as they went out before the army, and to say, Praise the LORD; for his mercy endureth for ever"* (2 Chron. 20:21).

The people of Judah went out to meet a mighty army from three enemy nations armed first and foremost with a praise song! In fact, the singers led the way—they weren't the backup choir; they were the main act!

Lord I praise you!

Wow thank for Jesus

And the Bible says, *"When they began to sing and to praise, the LORD set ambushments against the children of Ammon, Moab, and mount Seir...and they were smitten"* (2 Chron. 20:22).

They turned on each other in their confusion and slaughtered one another, all the while the singers and men of the army were singing and marching toward them. By the time the men of Judah showed up, they saw nothing but *"dead bodies fallen to the earth, and none escaped"* (v. 24). *I'm gonna sing and march*

It took Jehoshaphat and his people three days to strip away all the jewels and other bounty from the bodies of these enemy armies. And on the fourth day, they stood again before the Lord with great joy at all God had done. People from all over Judah came to Jerusalem with psalteries and harps and trumpets and gave God a tremendous offering of praise.

When facing an enemy...

- Don't have a pity party.

- Don't call your friends to come to you so you can cry on their shoulders.

- Don't get into the "blues" of depression.

- Don't wallow in your hurt feelings.

Start praising God! *Now Thurs -3.7-24 342 pm hallelujah!*

When praise goes up, power comes down...anointing comes down...deliverance comes down from God! *Praise is a weapon*

God Can Use "Even" You

Now what does all this have to do with Othniel, the first of the judges?

Othniel was from Judah. He was a man from a family steeped in praise and faith. He was a man with an uncle who believed, at age eighty-five, that he could take on a mountain full of giants and come out the winner. Othniel was a man with a clear understanding that he was from the tribe that is supposed to lead, supposed to praise, and supposed to be like a strong lion that captures its prey.

The day came in the lives of the Israelites where it wasn't only a matter of the general oppressive nature of the Canaanites, Hittites, Amorites, Perizzites, Hivites, and Jebusites that got to the Israelites.

The land was invaded by Mesopotamia—later, this area was called Babylonia, and parts of it became known as Assyria. This was the great kingdom to the northeast. To be invaded by Mesopotamia was to be seriously invaded!

The Mesopotamians, under the leadership of a man with a name almost too big to pronounce in one breath—Chushanrishathaim—took over Judah and the people of Israel served Chushanrishathaim for eight years (Judg. 4:8).

Now to say they served this man from Mesopotamia does not mean they waited on him with food and wine. To serve him meant that they became slaves. Chushanrishathaim took everything the Israelites had. He no doubt used the vast majority of what he took to support his invading army, which was probably headed south toward the conquest of Egypt. Anything left over would have been sent as tribute money back to Mesopotamia.

To "serve" Chushanrishathaim meant to be worked to death. It meant to be conscripted to hard labor to the point where every waking hour was spent in hard labor to produce something that never benefited the worker. The Israelites were utterly defeated.

And they cried to the Lord.

I personally don't know why it took them eight years. About eight days of that kind of treatment and I'd be willing to cry out to God. Nevertheless, the Israelites suffered for eight years, which no doubt seemed like an eternity to them.

And the Bible says that *"when the children of Israel cried unto the LORD, the LORD raised up a deliverer to the children of Israel, who delivered them, even Othniel the son of Kenaz, Caleb's younger brother"* (Judg. 3:9).

Othniel had some experience in war, but not much. He had been credited by Caleb with the defeat of a city named Kirjathsepher (renamed Debir by the Israelites). But the Bible says the judge raised up was *"even Othniel."* That's another way of saying, "Can you believe it was Othniel?" Nobody would have expected Othniel to be the one to lead a campaign against the powerful forces of Mesopotamia, and specifically the armies of Chushanrishathaim. Defeating the Canaanites in one city in southern Judah wasn't at all the same as taking on a mighty invading army from a powerful empire.

We in America today have virtually no idea what it means to bow before a powerful invading empire and to become slaves to that invading power. Something happens to the mind and heart of a people who are enslaved by an invading empire. Hope grows very dim. Human energy is sapped by the hard work that is laid upon a slave. Dignity is trampled upon.

No person can rise up out of that condition on his own. There simply is no pulling yourself up by your bootstraps, and I defy anyone who tries to tell you otherwise. Someone outside your own self has to speak to you words of hope and courage. There's no way you can muster up the strength to rise up in leadership on your own will and vision.

The Bible says…

"Even Othniel."

How many people can we look at today and say about them, "even" that person? We say it in different ways: "God is a great God—He's able to deliver even Tom from a drug problem." "God is able to save the worst sinner—why, He even saved Joe." "Who would have ever thought it—God healed even Mary who was at death's door with that terrible disease."

God seems to specialize in doing miracles that are at the extreme.

God can deliver even you.

God can deliver someone else through the likes of even you!

"Even" Othniel the nobody...

"Even" Othniel the bent-over slave under Mesopotamian domination...

"Even" Othniel was the one chosen by God.

God, however, never expected Othniel to take on Mesopotamia by his own power or even by the combined power of all the Israelites.

The Bible says, *"The Spirit of the LORD came upon him"* (Judg. 3:10).

Let me tell you, the Spirit of the Lord makes all the difference in a person's life.

No enemy is too great...

No bondage is too oppressive...

No evil is too mighty...

When the Spirit of the Lord comes upon a person.

Without the Spirit of the Lord, you are just a lump of clay filled with a lot of hot air, trying to do something you think should be done.

With the Spirit of the Lord, you are a powerful tool, functioning in all the wisdom and might necessary to do what God says is to be done.

The Anointing Makes All the Difference

When the Lord raised up Othniel and the Spirit of the Lord came upon this oppressed slave, things happened. The Bible tells us that he *"went out to war: and the LORD delivered Chushanrisha-thaim king of Mesopotamia into his hand; and his hand prevailed against Chushanrishathaim"* (Judg. 3:10).

One man, raised up in a small upstart kingdom, led God's people out of bondage to the prevailing world power of that day.

The land had rest from its enemies for forty years after Chushanrishathaim king of Mesopotamia was defeated.

Eight years of bondage. Forty years of rest.

No matter how long you have been in bondage, God has a rest ahead for you. He has a peace for your life, a laying down of the trouble, a relief from the pain.

There's no mention that Othniel ever had to defeat another enemy or make any other major decisions as a judge. As long as he was alive, the land had rest.

Praise led the way to total victory. It wiped out the enemy. It set up peace and prosperity. It freed the people from bondage.

The years that followed this victory were years of joy, of occupying the land and dwelling in it with a fullness of God's blessing.

Never discount the power of praise to bring about your deliverance.

And once you have experienced the delivering power of God, never stop praising Him.

That's where the Israelites made their mistake.

In the aftermath of this great victory and an entire generation of peace won through praise, we read that terrible repeating line in the book of Judges: *"And the children of Israel did evil again in the sight of the LORD"* (Judg 3:12).

So to me it is said Stop Stop speaking defeat stop judging only praise unto the LORD

6

You Are Designed to Bring God Glory

A fter Othniel died, the people fell into sin again. And this time, God allowed Eglon, the king of Moab, to come against Israel.

Eglon didn't come alone, though. He recruited the armies of the Ammonites and the Amalekites to join him. They struck Israel and took over a stronghold in the Promised Land—they captured and possessed the "city of palm trees." This refers to the site where Jericho had stood. A genuine city had not yet been built after the collapse of Jericho from the armies led by Joshua. Jericho was known for its palm trees, and the people who dwelled there lived mostly in tents while they rebuilt a city. Jericho is one of the oldest known cities in the history of the earth, probably because of its climate and ideal location near the Jordan River, and because the area was an oasis, surrounded by highly productive palm trees,.

The Moabites, with the Ammonites and Amalekites at their side, took over this prime location and claimed it as their own.

What the Israelites had won through a miracle—the tumbling of walls at the sound of a trumpet and shout of praise—they later lost through disobedience. *I don't want to be disobidut*

Three Powerful Invaders

Papa God hellp to do you will

Who were these invaders that were allowed to oppress the Israelites? They are not unlike the forces that oppress us today.

The Moabites

The Moabites were distant relatives to the Israelites. Lot, the nephew of Abraham, was led by angels to escape from Sodom and Gomorrah. Lot's wife turned back and became a pillar of salt, but Lot and his daughters fled to the hills east of the Dead Sea. They lived in caves there, just the three of them; they may not have known that anybody else on earth had survived that terrible rain of fire and brimstone from heaven. The daughters, fearful that their father would die one day and they would never marry or have children, took turns getting their father drunk and then lying with him to have sex with him. Both girls became pregnant by their father. The first girl named her baby boy "Moab," which literally means "from my father."

Moab was a great-nephew of Abraham, but Abraham never knew him and he didn't know Abraham. Moab became the founder of a group of people who occupied what is now a part of Jordan.

The Israelites had to move through this area of Moab as they moved north out of the wilderness and approached the Promised Land from the east. If you look at a map, you'll find the Arnon River flowing into the Dead Sea about a third of the way down on the Jordan side (east). This Arnon River was the northern border of Moab.

As the Israelites approached the territory of Moab, Balak, the king of Moab, hired the prophet Balaam to curse Israel, and when

Balaam refused to do so, Balak attempted to subdue the people by luring the Israelites into idolatry and immorality. (See Numbers 22–25.) A great plague broke out among the Israelites and they repented and returned to the Lord, but not before they experienced a tremendous loss of life. The move against the Israelites in the book of Judges may very well have been a preventative move on the part of the Moabites, who were very fearful of the size and prosperity of the twelve tribes.

The Ammonites

Who were the Ammonites? The second daughter of Lot had a son she named "Ben Ammi," and he was the founder of the Ammonites. Thus both the Moabites and the Ammonites came from Lot, the nephew of Abraham. The Ammonites occupied the territory just north of Moab (north of the Arnon River), which is the area just east across the Jordan River from Jericho.

The Ammonites had joined the Moabites in hiring Balaam to curse Israel. Because of this action, here's what God said about the Moabites and Ammonites:

> An Ammonite or Moabite shall not enter into the congregation of the Lord; even to their tenth generation shall they not enter into the congregation of the Lord for ever: because they met you not with bread and with water in the way, when ye came forth out of Egypt; and because they hired against thee Balaam the son of Beor of Pethor of Mesopotamia, to curse thee....Thou shalt not seek their peace nor their prosperity all thy days for ever.   (Deut. 23:3–4, 6)

The Israelites had not declared Moab and Ammon to be their enemies; God had declared them to be their enemies. He said, "Don't seek peace or good relations with them."

The Amalekites

The Moabites and Ammonites were joined by a group of Amalekites. These people are identified in the Bible as a clan descending from Esau. (See Genesis 36:15–16.) Esau, of course, was the older brother of Jacob who sold his birthright to Jacob for a bowl of lentil stew and also gave up his rightful blessing to Jacob.

The Amalekites were more nomadic than the Moabites and Ammonites. They wandered over a fairly wide area south of the Promised Land, including the Sinai and Arabian peninsulas. They were the first enemies to attack the Israelites under Moses at the great battle of Rephidim. (See Exodus 17:8–14.) The attack was totally without provocation.

This battle at Rephidim was the one in which Moses held up his rod—with the help of Aaron and Hur at his sides—and as long as Moses' rod was in the air, the Israelites prevailed. Joshua led this battle, and at the conclusion of it, which was a victory for the Israelites, the Lord said to Moses:

Write this for a memorial in a book, and rehearse it in the ears of Joshua: for I will utterly put out the remembrance of Amalek from under heaven. And Moses built an altar, and called the name of it Jehovahnissi: for he said, Because the Lord hath sworn that the Lord will have war with Amalek from generation to generation. (Exod. 17:14–16)

Again, I want you to see that these Amalekites were distant relatives of the Israelites. They became enemies of the Israelites because God declared them to be His enemies.

I'm giving you all this background to make this point: Sometimes the enemy that you need to be delivered from is an enemy that's right in your home territory. The enemy may even be in the form of your distant relatives or people of your own basic race or ethnicity.

The Enemy May Be Closer than You Think

Othniel had faced an invading army from a great empire to the northeast. This second wave of enemies came from next door—right across the Jordan River, right across the Dead Sea, and right across the southern border of Judah.

All our enemies aren't "other folk." Some of our enemies are "our folk."

Who is likely to have the greatest influence in dragging you down into sin? It's likely the friend you grew up with who convinces you to try something on a dare or to go with him or her "just this once" to "see what this is like."

Most prostitutes work for men in their own neighborhoods.

Most gang members associate with people who are their "homies"—the people who live closest to them.

Most drug users get their drugs from people they've known for years.

One of the great lures of temptation is the line, "You're one of us. So be like us! This is what we do, so this is what you should do."

If a purple and green monster from a distant planet landed in your neighborhood and tried to get you to take a substance that would make you lose control of your mind and your nervous system, you'd say "no" and run the other direction as fast as you could, trying to figure out as you ran what number you might call for help.

But if the guy who's just a couple of years older than you, who never finished high school but now drives a fancy car and dresses like a million dollars, and is somebody your friends think is cool, offers you a substance that makes you lose control of your mind and nervous system—that seems to be another story entirely!

The oppression that comes at the hand of a near neighbor, or even a blood relative, is no less than the oppression that comes from outside the neighborhood. In fact, it can be worse.

The Israelites were in bondage to Chushanrishathaim, king of Mesopotamia, for only eight years. They served Eglon the king of Moab for eighteen years. (See Judges 3:14.)

Perhaps it was because the Moabites were distant relatives; perhaps the oppression wasn't quite as severe; or perhaps the oppression still allowed some cultural similarities—we do not know the exact reason, but it took more than twice as long for the Israelites to come to their senses and cry out to God in repentance.

Eighteen years—time for a new generation to be born and raised—passed before the Israelites cried out the Lord.

The good news is that when they cried out, God once again raised up a deliverer.

A Left-Handed Man Named Ehud

This time the deliverer God chose was Ehud, the son of Gera. He was not from the tribe of Judah, but from the tribe of Benjamin, the smallest of the tribes. He was a left-handed man, which made him somewhat unusual among the Israelites as a whole, but not unusual among the Benjamites. All of the left-handed men mentioned in the Bible are from the tribe of Benjamin, which is somewhat ironic since the word *Benjamin* literally means "son of the right hand". It was precisely this unusual trait that qualified Ehud for the task God had for him.

Let me pause to point out that God can use the unusual aspect of your life to bring Him great glory. There's no natural trait or attribute that stands in the way of your being used by God. No person is ever too ugly, has feet too big, is too tall or too short, or too fat or too thin, or too anything else to be used by God. God uses people in all shapes and forms, all races and ethnicities, all backgrounds and traits, all abilities and talents. The trait that makes you unusual may very well be the point where you need to begin your ministry.

We know this to be true, of course, when it comes to outstanding traits that we see as positive—a person is exceptionally beautiful or handsome, exceptionally talented as a singer or musician, exceptionally bright or good with his hands. We also need to see this about the traits that we may not like or that we believe limit us in some way. The exact opposite may be God's truth. We all know about the comedian who had a large nose—and made it his trademark; the country singer who stuttered badly—and made it his calling card; the tall and ugly man who seems to show up as the monster in every movie that needs a monster.

God has made you uniquely you—one of a kind with no other person like you on the earth today or ever in history. He built into you all the unique aspects that make you distinctive and that He intends for you to use for His glory. Don't shrink back from those things that set you apart from other people. Be God's witness just as you are!

Here's what happened in the case of Ehud.

Ehud was chosen by the children of Israel to deliver a present to Eglon, king of Moab, who was staying at the summer palace that the Moabites had built for him north of Jericho, near Gilgal. Actually the present was probably a sum of money that represented their taxes or their tribute money.

Ehud presented the tribute money to the king and then he dismissed the men who had come with him to carry the containers of tribute money. He also left the king's presence, and, traveling alone, he made it about as far as the quarries that were outside the city of Gilgal. Then, he returned to the king's palace and said, *"I have a secret errand unto thee, O king"* (Judg. 3:19). The implication was that he had a secret word from God just for the king.

A Turn-Around Experience

Let me tell you a little about this area of the Promised Land.

Gilgal is a small city northwest of Jericho in the area given to the tribe of Ephraim. It is just north of the tribe of Benjamin. Also in Ephraim is the city of Shiloh, which is where the tabernacle was brought and permanently placed after the Israelites had claimed the land and before the temple was built in Jerusalem. The area was known for hosting many pilgrims who came to worship God in the outer court of the tabernacle, including the sacrifices they brought to the tabernacle. Under Eglon and the Moabites, Ephraim also very likely became a center for worship of the Moabite gods and the statues built to them.

The Bible tells us that when Ehud left Eglon's presence, he had traveled as far as the quarries before he turned around. The stone from these quarries was used to carve images of the false gods worshipped by the Moabites! It is very likely that a number of these images were at the quarry site awaiting pickup and delivery to other territories dominated by Moab.

Ehud came face to face with the images of false gods, in a territory traditionally known as being holy to God Almighty. That must have been a powerful moment in his life. The Bible doesn't say this directly, but the implication is very strong that Ehud saw these images and made an immediate decision and commitment that the time had come for him to follow through on a plan he had made even before he had left home with the tribute money.

Your Skills Are Your Weapons

The Bible tells us that Ehud had made a two-edged dagger for himself—something that would have been difficult for him to do given the resources available to him under Moabite domination. Just to buy the materials would have taken a great deal of time. To make the dagger and sharpen the blades would have taken more time. Ehud may not have known when or how he was going to use this dagger, but God had put it in his heart to make it.

87

I don't know what talent God has given you, but I do know this—whatever talent you possess, God expects you to sharpen that talent into a perfected skill. singing write songs play uknle, n

Your skills—developed out of your God-given talents—are what God is likely to use to help you sustain your deliverance.

It is God who anoints us with courage and gives us direction and empowers us to develop and use our skills. But it is up to us to turn talents into skills through education and practice and experience.

Skills are needed in jobs; skills and jobs deliver us from poverty.

Skills often put us into relationships with people who can help us develop even greater and more varied skills; skills produce the income that pays the bills of those who advise us financially and the taxes of the public servants who teach our children and keep our neighborhoods safe.

Skills can give us entrance into many parts of the world to preach the Gospel. Some of the most difficult parts of the world to reach with the Gospel are the Muslim-dominated, oil-producing countries. None of those nations allows Christian missionaries to gain entrance. Who gets to go in? People who have skills in drilling for oil and managing refineries.

Skills—and specifically the skills of reading and writing—help us proclaim the Gospel to all people.

I don't know what idea or dream God has given you—a dream that results in excellence and deliverance and righteousness—but I do know that any dream God gives you is a dream that God expects you to keep over time and to treasure in your heart. He expects you to get ready for the day that He allows that dream to burst forth into a reality. He expects you to do everything you need to do to be prepared for the hour and day and month and year in which God brings you forth to do His holy work.

Ehud had likely owned that dagger for years, and he took it with him on his trip to deliver tribute money to Eglon. The dagger was about a cubit in length—but this isn't the normal word for cubit that is used in other parts of the Bible. This word for cubit means the dagger was probably nine or ten inches long. He hid it inside his garments under his right thigh.

Let me quickly point out that this was not the normal place for a person to hide a weapon of this type. The normal place would be to hide a weapon on the left thigh so a right-handed person could reach across the body and pull it out of its sheath and immediately slash or drive the dagger into a person with a strong "backhanded" motion. But remember, Ehud is left-handed.

God puts such details into His Word for a reason—He wants us to see that no detail is too trivial for Him to notice or use.

When Ehud got as far as Gilgal and he saw those carved images to false gods, something inside of him began to churn. He no doubt felt a righteous indignation fueled by anger at the years of bondage in which his people had been living. He turned around and went back to visit king Eglon.

When Ehud showed up telling Eglon that he had a secret message for him from the Lord, the king was eager to hear it. He sent all of his bodyguards out of the room. And they left. They no doubt had checked out Ehud, and they knew he was just a poor Benjamite coming to pay his taxes. They knew what to look for in the way of hidden weapons, and where to look for hidden weapons, and they didn't suspect Ehud in the least.

Eglon was sitting in the summer parlor of the palace—a place that was reserved only for his use. These summer parlors were usually built in a garden with as much shade as possible from various trees, and they were usually on a second-floor level that could be reached only by stairs. The two or three rooms and terraces of a summer parlor were a private luxury—they were a place to get out of the heat of the day and enjoy whatever cool breezes might be blowing.

Eglon was eager to hear the secret message that Ehud claimed to have. Eglon, no doubt, had heard enough about the God of Israel to be curious about Him. He, no doubt, was familiar with the tabernacle at Shiloh just a few miles away, although the worship rituals there were a mystery to him. He was very likely a superstitious man who was eager for supernatural signs—that seems to be a mark of all the Moabite kings mentioned in the Bible.

He didn't think it at all strange that Ehud got up out of his chair and approached the king as if to tell him a secret in a whisper or very low voice. That was to be expected in the sharing of a "holy" secret.

As Ehud got close to the king, whom the Bible describes as *"a very fat man"* (Judg. 3:17), Ehud reached down and pulled out his dagger, and with a powerful thrust he drove that dagger upward into the king's belly. He thrust it with such force that the entire dagger ended up inside Eglon's body! The Bible says, *"The fat closed upon the blade, so that he could not draw the dagger out of his belly; and the dirt came out"* (v. 22). The contents of Eglon's abdomen and intestines began to spill out onto the floor—in other words, the dung of his body came gushing out. Yes, the Bible has that kind of graphic detail!

Ehud turned and went out through the porch, shut the doors of the parlor behind him and locked them, and then made his escape. The bodyguards may even have seen him go, but they didn't think anything of that—it just meant Ehud's audience with the king was over.

The king's servants went upstairs and when they saw the doors of the parlor were locked, they said, "The king is probably in the bathroom chamber." Locked doors were a sign of privacy even then, and given the stench that was no doubt coming from that room, it was reasonable for the servants to assume the king was in the bathroom.

So the servants of Eglon waited...and waited...and waited. They waited until they were *"ashamed"* (v. 25)—which means they waited until they were willing to risk shaming themselves for interrupting a king who might be relieving himself. They got no answer from the king when they called to him, and eventually when they took a key and opened the doors, they found their king dead.

A Rallying Cry for Battle

Meanwhile, all this delay had given Ehud plenty of time to escape. He had traveled well past the quarries by the time the bodyguards found dead king Eglon. Ehud went to Seirath, a town close to Gilgal, and there he blew a trumpet in the mountain of Ephraim, and all of the children of Israel joined him.

To blow a trumpet meant to send word to all the tribes to gather together for a war conference. Under the rule of the Moabites, those who left their work and went to such a meeting were in grave danger. Nevertheless, the leaders of the people rallied to Ehud.

Ehud said to them, *"Follow after me: for the LORD hath delivered your enemies the Moabites into your hand. And they went down after him, and took the fords of Jordan toward Moab, and suffered not a man to pass over"* (Judg. 3:28).

They took control of the river crossing and didn't allow any person from Moab to come into the Promised Land, and they also stopped Moabites from fleeing the Promised Land and seeking refuge in their home nation. Some ten thousand able-bodied Moabites were killed in the battle, all of them called *"men of valour"* (v. 29), which means they were skilled and courageous soldiers.

In the natural, ten thousand able-bodied, skilled, and courageous soldiers should have been able to wipe out a ragtag band of Israelites. After all, the Israelites were a people who had been under their strong dominion for eighteen years, people who hadn't been united as an army, people who didn't have weaponry or defensive posts. But when the spirit of the Lord is on your side—oh, yes, when the spirit of the Lord is on your side—nothing can stand in your way.

The Bible says, *"Moab was subdued that day"* (v. 30). The deliverance wasn't a prolonged, drawn-out process. It happened very quickly.

That hope is always there for you and me. Things can turn around in your life in a day, in an hour. The rebuilding time is often a process over time. The actions of God, however, are definitive and swift.

In the aftermath of this great victory against Moab, the land had rest for eighty years. This is the longest period of peace mentioned in the history of the Israelites. Two generations of people lived and died without war.

The Victory God Has for You

Let me ask you today:

What might God do through you and in you to bring glory to His name?

God doesn't want you living with that fear you have...

Or that phobia...

Or that doubt...

Or that addiction...

Or that lack of needed resources...

Or that trouble...

Or that disease.

Nothing about your poverty, sickness, emotional weakness, addiction, or trouble brings Him glory except your giving God praise in the midst of your trial. God gets the greatest glory when you are delivered from whatever is holding you back, pushing you down, or rolling over you.

What is it that God desires to do in you, for you, and through you?

Do you have a clear understanding that God wants to bring you to the fullness and freedom of living in His blessings?

You were created and designed to bring God glory.

Never lose sight of that eternal fact.

Today Papa God Thursday 3-7-2024
I ask you to fill me with you will ?
desire to do you will from this moment
on 7:24 pm. Take full controll holy spirit
dont let me go I need you I give my
desire of you will the talent that you
gave me for your Glory. Singing
Serving playing the ukulei lei muscie
whatever you will Papa use it for
you Glory. Lord I praise You

7

Use What You Have in Your Hand

The third judge of Israel is given only one verse in the book of Judges. But oh, the things we can learn from that one verse!

This judge whom God raised up was named Shamgar. He was the son of Anath. He may have been a judge of Israel simultaneously with Ehud. Since a judge was a leader who brought deliverance to the people, there certainly could have been more than one judge at a time. Shamgar is credited with killing six hundred Philistines, which certainly must have brought deliverance to those who were under Philistine oppression!

We read about the Philistines again and again in the Bible. Who were these people who so sorely oppressed the Israelites?

The Philistines originally came from Caphtor, which is ancient Crete. (See Genesis 10:13–14; Jeremiah 47:4; Amos 9:7.) A large trading colony of the Minoans, which was the culture that flourished on Crete for about fourteen hundred years, was established at Gerar in the time of Abraham. (See Genesis 21:22–34.) Centuries later, there came a time when both the Egyptian empire to the south and the Hittites who had been the major power from the north grew weak, and an invasion of "Sea Peoples" was launched from Libya against the southern coast of the Promised Land. Hieroglyphics in Egypt tell the story of this massive land and sea invasion that came across the Nile Delta from the north, which would be the southern area of the Promised Land. Egyptian forces, under the great pharaoh Ramses III, pushed the invaders back but allowed them to settle along the coast and to establish five major cities: Ashdod, Ashkelon, Ekron, Gath, and Gaza.

From these cities along the coast, the Philistines penetrated deep into the Promised Land, going as far north as Hazor and Dan, and as far west as southern Galilee, Bethel, and Jerusalem.

Each of the five cities of the Philistines had its own ruler, but the five rulers acted together as a ruling council. The rulers also acted as military leaders in war so that their efforts would be coordinated.

The first time that the Philistines are mentioned as a force coming against the Israelites is during the time of Shamgar, but they remained a formidable force against the Israelites for hundreds of years. Samson confronted the Philistines. David confronted Goliath, a giant of the Philistines. In fact, David fought the Philistines repeatedly. The Philistines came against the armies of kings Jehoram, Uzziah, and Hezekiah, and the prophets Amos and Isaiah both spoke against them.

The Philistines were not worshippers of Baal. Rather, their chief god was called Dagon. They also had a female goddess whom they called simply "Great Mother."

The Philistines were warriors—fighters, invaders, pursuers, conquerors, dominators. They were always pushing in whatever direction they could push. They were always in search of a conquest.

The amazing feat of Shamgar is that he killed six hundred of these powerful Philistines with an ox goad, which is little more than a stick!

An ox goad is a pole about eight feet long and about two inches in diameter. On one end was a sharp point for pricking oxen when their movements became too slow or they were headed in the wrong direction. At the other end of the pole was a sharp chisel-like blade that was used to clean a plowshare of any weeds, roots, thorns, or hard clay that might get stuck to it.

At no other time in the Bible do we find an ox goad being used as a weapon, much less a weapon used to kill six hundred enemy men. Again, God used the unusual to do the miraculous. Just think about it. God used a farm boy with a stick—a man accustomed to following oxen as they plowed a field—to become a mighty warrior and deliverer.

Anything you have in your hand God can transform into something He uses for good. So let me ask you: "What do you have in your hand?"

What is your hand possessing?

What is your hand holding?

What is within your grasp?

It's when you open your hand and give that thing you are holding to God that God can take it and use it in a miraculous way to deliver you or others. The information of this Bible

God will not pry open your hand to take from you what you do not want to yield or submit to Him. *You* must do the yielding. *You* must do the giving. God's part is to take what you submit and to sift it and sort it and subdue it and put it back into your hand as a weapon of power.

I recently heard a story about a young couple who had lost everything in bankruptcy court. They had only the clothes on their backs and their wedding rings on their fingers.

They came to a point in their lives where they knew that it was their greed that had caused them to run up their credit cards and acquire bills they couldn't pay. They humbly cried out to God with a sincere heart and said, "Lord, we were wrong. Please forgive us and deliver us."

God called upon that young couple to give their wedding rings to Him. The rings were the last thing of value they owned, but they both knew that God had spoken to them individually, and they agreed as a couple that this was something they were to do in obedience to God. When they put their wedding rings into the offering basket as it passed them in the pew, they were truly submitting their entire lives to God.

What happened?

The man who was taking up the offering that morning saw what this young couple did. He knew a little about their story, and he saw their commitment to the Lord shining on their faces as they offered their gift. He went to the young man after the service and asked him if he needed a job. The young man said, "I have a job, but I'd certainly be open to a better job." The man offered him a better job, and he took it.

This young man and his wife went to financial counseling together as well as to marriage counseling. They emerged from all that counseling twelve months later with their bills paid, money in savings, and a down payment on a house. God kept their marriage strong as they rebuilt their lives. Two years after they had given their wedding rings to God as a sign of their total surrender to Him, they had a service at the church, in which they renewed their vows and exchanged new rings—and this time there was a diamond in each ring!

The good news is that those rings with diamonds were fully paid for, as were all their other bills.

They not only learned and grew as a couple, but in the process, this young family was also delivered from debt. They don't use credit cards now. They don't buy things "on time"; they pay cash, they have a savings account, they have an investments account, they have good-paying jobs, they have a home, and they have deep joy in their hearts because they tithe their money and give offerings on top of that.

Another man I know had cigarettes in his hand. In fact, for years, I never saw this man when he didn't have a cigarette in his hand—either lit or about to be lit. He was addicted to nicotine and had been since he was a young teenager.

One day he opened his hand and gave God that packet of cigarettes. He walked down to the altar of the church he attended and laid the cigarettes there and walked away.

God didn't give this man a packet of cigarettes back. Instead, He put a hammer in his hand. He called this man to a volunteer ministry of fixing up the homes of the elderly poor people who lived near the church. Many of them lived in homes that had fallen into disrepair over the years. This man became part of a team of men that worked evenings and on weekends to rebuild and repair walls, roofs, fences, doors, porches, steps—you name it.

This man discovered that you can't hammer nails and smoke at the same time. During breaks, the men on the team would talk and eat, but never smoke. Over time, this man's desire for tobacco completely left him. God had taken what this man gave to him and returned to his hand a weapon for his deliverance. He said, "When I've got that hammer in my hand, I'm helping build up another person's life—not just their home, but their esteem and their faith and their encouragement that somebody in God's church loves them. When I had cigarettes in my hand, I was tearing down a person's life—my life! I was tearing down my health and my future. God took what had me in bondage and gave me something in its place that brings deliverance."

There's yet another interesting aspect of this man's story. This man calculated one day how much money he had spent in a year on cigarettes. After he had been involved in the building ministry for a year, he totaled up what he had spent personally on nails and screws and other supplies and tools. It was just about the same amount, give or take a dollar or two! He said, "I was smoking something that was driving nails in my own coffin. As part of the building team, I was driving nails to bring new life to a home!"

What is it that you have in your hand today?

What is in it that God wants to redeem and use, not only for your deliverance, but also to help bring deliverance to others?

Three Great Lessons from the First Three Judges

I believe there are three great lessons we can take away from the lives of these first three judges.

First, it's not your need or your suffering that compels God to deliver you. It's your calling out to God with a repentant heart and a total reliance on Him. *Please Papa God I need you*

People often say, "There's so much suffering in the world. Why does God allow all that suffering?" One of the reasons is that the people who are suffering aren't crying out to God for deliverance. They aren't crying out in repentance, humbly confessing that they have idols or that they are worshipping a false god. They aren't crying out in their faith, trusting God to be God in their lives, willing to submit all and surrender all to Him.

It's not the depth of our suffering or our need that prompts God to act. It's the depth of our desire to turn back to Him and worship Him. It's our faith in God that causes God to move mountains on our behalf.

Second, it's not your position or status that brings about your deliverance. Othniel, "even Othniel," was a relative of Caleb and a victorious warrior in the past—but as a slave for eight years, he had no claim to fame. Ehud was a left-handed man from the smallest of the tribes. Shamgar was a farm boy. None of these men had privilege, status, wealth, fame, good looks, or physical power on their side—at least not to any degree that it is mentioned in the Bible as a defining trait.

No, these were ordinary men whom God chose to use in an extraordinary way. He put His Spirit on them for His purposes and His glory, not for their purposes or their glory.

The only thing that qualifies you to do anything of note in the spiritual realm is your relationship with Jesus Christ. On your own, you can't do anything. With Christ Jesus, you can do all things as the Spirit guides and empowers you.

Third, it's never the weapon that matters in a victory. We don't know the precise weapons that Othniel used, but the traditional weapons at that time were the sword and shield, and that is likely what Othniel had in battling the king of Mesopotamia. Ehud used a dagger. Shamgar had an ox goad as his weapon.

It's not the weapon that matters.

What matters is faith in your heart, a willingness to be delivered and to bring deliverance to others, courage to fight the fight, and a desire to love God and obey Him with your entire being.

*Hallelujah
I have Papa God my Jesus & the holy spirit. God's word the sword of the spirit. I love you Papa God.*

8

Your Destiny in the Land: Freedom from Bondage

The Bible has a wonderful line of poetry that states:

They fought from heaven; the stars in their courses fought against Sisera. (Judg. 5:20)

I am not a student of astronomy and I would never attempt to stand before an audience and name the galaxies and stars. But I do know this: The stars were hung in space by the same Creator who made you and me. They were designed to be in the exact place and orbit in which they are found in the night sky. They were positioned with precision in the universe.

The same is true for you and me. God has a plan for your life and mine. He has an orbit in which we move through our lives. He has positioned us with precision in the exact time and place where we live and move and have our being in Christ Jesus.

I also know this:

- If you battle against God's plan and God's design, you will always be defeated.

- If you rebel against God's plan, you will experience failure.

The children of Israel once again turned to idols and false gods after Ehud and Shamgar. The Bible says:

And the children of Israel again did evil in the sight of the Lord, when Ehud was dead. And the Lord sold them into the hand of Jabin king of Canaan, that reigned in Hazor; the captain of whose host was Sisera, which dwelt in Harosheth of the Gentiles. And the children of Israel cried unto the Lord: for he had nine hundred chariots of iron; and twenty years he mightily oppressed the children of Israel. (Judg. 4:1–3)

Notice that once again, *"the children of Israel cried unto the Lord."* This time their cries came after twenty years of oppression. And this time, the enemy was Jabin, king of Canaan, who reigned in Hazor. Hazor was in the north of the Promised Land in the territory assigned to the tribe of Naphtali.

Now, this isn't the only time Hazor is mentioned in the Bible. And it isn't the only time we find the name *Jabin* referring to the king of Hazor.

Another Jabin—one who had lived more than a hundred years before this Jabin—was king of Hazor in the time of Joshua. He joined with three other Canaanite kings—the kings of Madon, Shimron, and Achshaph—as well as the kings of the Canaanite tribes that lived to the east and west, including some Amorites, Hittites, Perizzites, and Jebusites, and they all fought against the Israelites near a place called Merom. The Lord said to Joshua, *"Be not afraid because of them: for to morrow about this time will I deliver them up all slain before Israel: thou shalt hock* [which means hamstring] *their horses, and burn their chariots with fire"* (Josh. 11:6).

Joshua and the people rose up the next morning and it all happened just as the Lord said. The Bible says the *"the LORD delivered them"* and after there were none remaining, Joshua *"hocked their horses, and burnt their chariots with fire"* (Josh. 11:8–9).

Then Joshua turned back and took Hazor and killed the first king Jabin with the sword. Hazor was the center for all the Canaanite kings so this was a great blow. Joshua took all the cities of those kings, and the kings themselves, and killed them with the sword. He burned Hazor, and the children of Israel took the spoil and livestock of all those cities.

Now it's a little more than a hundred years later. The Canaanites have been allowed to regroup and rebuild Hazor and remake chariots. There's another king Jabin on the Canaanite throne. This Jabin has a powerful general named Sisera in charge of his army. The army has nine hundred chariots of iron, and they begin to rule the roads in the northern part of the Promised Land. They completely controlled all trade and travel over those roads. They ran down anybody who tried to confront them.

What a picture this is of what happens to some people in the church! They come to Christ and are saved, are filled with the Holy Spirit, and begin to follow the Lord in their lives. They know God has driven out certain sinful habits and tendencies from their lives—in fact, those habits have been thoroughly hamstrung, burned, or killed. But then, those habits suddenly seem to emerge in a strength of force that is even greater than originally experienced.

What happens in these cases?

The people who were delivered from sinful desires at the beginning of their walk with the Lord stopped "putting off" the old man and "putting on the new man" with the same diligence and awareness they initially had. They let down their guard. They didn't continue to be alert to the ways in which the devil had once tripped them up. They thought they were immune to certain forces and temptations—only to discover that they were not at all immune to them.

None of Us Is Immune to Temptation

The Bible tells us that every person struggles with *"the lust of the flesh, and the lust of the eyes, and the pride of life"* (1 John 2:16). These are things that are *"in the world,"* and we Christians live in the world, even though we are not *"of the world."* We never stop being confronted with the things of the world.

The lust of the flesh is always going to be there. If the devil has tempted you into sexual sin in the past, he doesn't give up on that temptation just because you confess Christ. You are changed—you are empowered by the Holy Spirit to resist that temptation with a new degree of strength—but the devil hasn't changed. He bides his time, just waiting for the moment when he can tempt you once again.

The lust of the eyes is always going to be there in the world. If the devil has tempted you in the past with the acquisition of things, he doesn't give up on that temptation just because you are filled with the Holy Spirit. The Holy Spirit gives you power to withstand the impulses associated with greed and control and the acquisition of "stuff" that a person associates with self-esteem and self-value. But the devil hasn't changed. He just waits, knowing that he'll have other opportunities to tempt you with the things of this world.

The pride of life is always part of this world. If the devil has tempted you in the past with a desire for fame and recognition and authority and being number one, he'll come again with those temptations. You may have changed—truly, the Holy Spirit gives you the power to become a servant rather than seeking to be a king—but the devil hasn't changed. He knows that weakness exists in the human heart.

We must always be on guard against these forces that are deeply rooted in our human nature.

What we tend to do, however, is to say to ourselves, "I'm strong enough now to withstand that temptation. I can watch those R- and X-rated movies now and not be tempted in the flesh. I can go to those parties or into those environments where the very atmosphere is one of sexual innuendo, and I will not even notice. I can look at those magazines and ignore the pictures and read only the articles."

If that's your line, you are fooling yourself! You may not give in to the temptation to commit sexual sin the first time you see a lewd movie or look at a pornographic web site you find on the computer. But some do—and you may—and I can guarantee you that if you allow that habit to grow back in your soul, you will eventually fall to that temptation. I don't care how long you've been a sanctified Christian. If you allow one chariot to be built, one part of Hazor to be built back...then another chariot to be built and another part of Hazor to be built back...then yet another chariot to be built and another part of Hazor to be built back...then one day you are going to find yourself overrun by the chariots sent out by a king Jabin in Hazor!

Well, you say, I need this particular purchase because it will make me look better as I attempt to make a sale. It may be the car you think you need to drive in order to sell real estate, or it may be the purchase of a house in the neighborhood in which you think you need to live in order to be in the "right crowd" for a career move, or it may be the purchase of a boat so you can float on the same lake as people who are the "kind" of people you want your son or daughter to marry. There's always an excuse for giving in to the *"lust of the eyes."*

When you start down that road—buying things in order to give yourself an identity and status—you are just allowing one chariot after the next to be built. The day will come when the devil will tempt you with something that will defeat you and ensnare you to the point where you are oppressed.

The same applies to the pride of life. If you begin to strive for just a little bit more recognition—a little bit more appreciation, a little bit more power and authority—you set yourself into a habit pattern that will result in your bondage.

It doesn't happen overnight. It happens bit by bit, one chariot and horse at a time, one stone on top of the next until Hazor is rebuilt; one move away from the Lord's best and into the flesh after one move, after one more move. And the bondage that results can last a very long time.

The negative consequences of an illicit affair can last the lifetime of a child conceived in that ungodly relationship. The devastation of divorce or estrangement related to sexual sin can produce yet another generation of sexual sin, not to mention a host of other emotional problems. The negative consequences of an ungodly sexual association can result in years of sickness and struggle against a deadly sexual disease.

The negative consequences of overspending and over-acquiring can result in years and years of debt, or years and years of recovering from bankruptcy.

The negative consequences of pursuing your own number-one interests can result in years of loneliness and a life void of genuine friendships and love.

If that's your story, don't wait another moment. Cry out to God in your bondage and own up to the fact that you have allowed another Jabin to become king, another Hazor to be built, another army of horses and chariots to roam your promised land. Confess your sin and ask God to raise up a deliverer on your behalf.

Don't Focus on the Enemy's Strength

The one prevailing fact that caused the Israelites the most pain appears to be the fact that Jabin *"had nine hundred chariots of iron"* (Judg. 4:3).

Nine hundred chariots! That would be like having nine hundred small tanks today—and all of those tanks roaming around an area about forty miles square! It's no wonder that fear gripped the heart of the Israelites.

Sometimes it seems that the opposition has all the strength. But that's because we only look at the things we can see, touch, and perceive with our senses. In the face of nine hundred chariots, Israel had no chance...in the natural.

You may be the person who has the least seniority in your department...in the natural, you have no chance of promotion.

You may be the person with the least education of all those in the room...in the natural, you have no chance of being the one whose opinion is heard and acted upon.

You may be the least powerful person in the room...in the natural, you may have no chance of being vindicated.

We do not, however, live in the natural realm alone. As sons and daughters of Almighty God, believers in the Lord Jesus Christ, and people who are filled with God's Holy Spirit, we do not deal with "chances." We deal in certainties that are rooted in an unshakable faith that God can and God will provide for His people!

In the supernatural, Jabin and Sisera and their nine hundred chariots didn't have a chance!

Anytime you are facing impossible odds, it's time for you to catch another glimpse of the strength that is on your side.

1 God has resources you don't know about.

2 God has ways you don't know.

3 God has methods you haven't even thought to use.

4 God has a plan He may not have revealed to you.

5 Trust the unlimited God to take on your limited problem!

6 One of the great stories in the Old Testament is a story about Elisha and his servant. They had gone to the city of Dothan and the

enemy of Elisha, the king of Syria, sent his armies to surround the city. Elisha's servant got up early the next morning and saw that the city was surrounded on all sides by a great army with horses and chariots. He came back to Elisha and said, *"Alas, my master! how shall we do?"* (2 Kings 6:15).

Elisha calmly answered, *"Fear not: for they that be with us are more than they that be with them"* (v. 16).

Then Elisha prayed and said, *"LORD, I pray thee, open his eyes, that he may see"* (v. 17). The Lord opened the eyes of the young man so he could see into the spiritual realm, and he saw the mountains around that city filled with horses and chariots of fire.

The force on the side of Elisha was exceedingly, abundantly greater than any force that a king of Syria might put together. (See 2 Kings 6:8–17.) God was in charge of that situation!

Ask the Lord today to open your eyes to His ability and His power. They are unlimited! God's ability and power are so vastly bigger than your problem that there's no comparison. You cannot compare the infinite with the finite—there's no equation known to mathematics to make that comparison.

A Woman Judge Named Deborah

It took twenty years of oppression, but the children of Israel finally *"cried unto the LORD."* And the judge God raised up for the deliverance of the Israelites was a woman named Deborah.

Deborah is described as a prophetess and the wife of Lapidoth. The Bible tells us that she dwelt under a palm tree between Ramah and Beth-el in mount Ephraim. In other words, she lived at an oasis many miles south of Naphtali. In fact, the tribes of Issachar and part of Manasseh were between Ephraim and Naphtali.

There, in the palm trees by her home, Deborah recounted to the Israelites the commands of God and gave the judgments of God as the Spirit moved in her life.

One day, Deborah received a word from the Lord about Barak, the son of Abinoam, who lived in Kedeshnaphtali. She sent word to him:

Hath not the LORD God of Israel commanded, saying, Go and draw toward mount Tabor, and take with thee ten thousand men of the children of Naphtali and of the children of Zebulun? And I will draw unto thee to the river Kishon Sisera, the captain of Jabin's army, with his chariots and his multitude; and I will deliver him into thine hand.
(Judg. 4:6–7)

Deborah wasn't telling Barak something he didn't know. The Lord had already told Barak exactly what to do and where to go. He had given him the full battle plan and had promised to deliver the oppressing army of the Canaanites into the hands of the Israelites under Barak's leadership. Barak knew his destiny in the Lord!

Barak knew, but he didn't act.

I truly believe that Barak was called to be a judge of Israel—he knew he was called. He didn't become a judge of Israel because he caved in to fear and didn't accept God's call on his life.

The Lord revealed to Deborah what He had destined for Barak. She sent word to him, many miles away, saying, "I know what you know. *'Hath not the LORD God of Israel commanded'* you?"

Deborah knew that God had a plan for deliverance. Deborah knew that Sisera was a defeated foe. She knew it just as assuredly as she knew God had hung the stars in space.

Barak sent back word, *"If thou wilt go with me, then I will go: but if thou wilt not go with me, then I will not go"* (Judg. 4:8).

The prophetess and judge Deborah agreed to go with Barak, but she let him know in advance that he wouldn't get any of the honor for the victory—rather, God would turn Sisera over to a woman.

I grow weary of men who complain about women who take leadership roles in the church. If a man would rise up and take on those roles, a woman wouldn't have to! But if a man doesn't have the courage to do what God calls him to do, a woman has every right to lead that prayer meeting or teach that Bible lesson or give that sermon that lifts up Jesus.

Barak called the men of Zebulun and Naphtali to Kedesh, and with the ten thousand men who answered the call, he moved toward Mount Tabor. Sisera quickly got word of this movement of Israelites—ten thousand people on foot moving toward one location could hardly be ignored—and he gathered together all of his chariots and horses of iron, as well as an untold number of foot soldiers.

Deborah again heard from the Lord and said to Barak, *"Up; for this is the day in which the Lord hath delivered Sisera into thine hand: is not the Lord gone out before thee?"* (Judg. 4:14). Barak heeded her word from the Lord and began to move down the mountain toward the plain where those nine hundred chariots and horses and thousands more foot soldiers were massed and waiting.

And here's what happened. The Bible tells us that *"the Lord discomfited Sisera"* (v. 15). *"Discomfited"* is an Old English word for "defeated." The Lord did it, and He did it in a most unusual way. The next chapter of Judges, which is the poetic version of the historical account, tells more details.

The Kishon River that runs through the valley between Mount Tabor and Megiddo flooded. Apparently there was a great rainstorm, and this otherwise almost-dry creek bed turned into a raging river that flooded a widespread area, turning this valley into a valley of mud. The iron chariots got bogged down in the mud. The horses, unable to free themselves from the chariots, began to go wild and reared and assaulted and killed many of the soldiers who tried to free them or help them. The soldiers began to flee on foot from their mud-bound chariots away from the river and toward Mount Tabor, where Barak and his men were just waiting for them on dry ground.

The account in Judges 5 says:

They fought from heaven; the stars in their courses fought against Sisera. The river of Kishon swept them away, that ancient river, the river Kishon. O my soul, thou hast trodden down strength. Then were the horsehoofs broken by the means of the prancings, the prancings of their mighty ones.
(Judg. 5:20–22)

When Jabin sent out Sisera to fight the Israelites, Sisera had already lost because he was taking on the God who made the stars!

This same God who made the stars is the God we serve!

What can an enemy do in the face of a God who makes stars, clusters together galaxies of stars, hangs them in space, and causes them to spin and move according to a precise plan?

What can an enemy do in the face of a God who orders all things, knows all things, sees all things, speaks what He wills, and goes where He wants?

God sent a fierce thunderstorm. He caused a flood where the day before the ground had been dry.

God has all the forces of nature under His control. On various occasions in the Bible, God used hailstones and wind and earthquakes to accomplish His purposes. The forces of nature, unleashed in fury, are no match for any person—they certainly are no match for an army of heavy iron chariots and horses.

God also has people—sometimes in strange places and with strange backgrounds—whom He uses for His purposes.

Sisera Hadn't Counted on Jael!

The general of the army, Sisera, fled from his chariot even as the other soldiers in his army fled from their chariots in the rising tide of raging waters. On foot, Sisera stumbled along in the mud and then on dry ground until he came to the tent of a nomadic family. He specifically sought refuge in the tent of Jael, the wife of Heber the Kenite. Heber the Kenite had separated himself from the rest of the Kenites and had set up his tent in the plain of Zaanaim, which is by Kedesh. (See Judges 4:11.) As was customary in that time, several tents were usually set up for a family. If there was more than one wife to the man, each wife had her own tent. We don't know if that was the case here, but Sisera went into the tent of Jael, wife of Heber.

Sisera thought he was safe. Jabin, the king of Hazor, and Heber the Kenite had a peace treaty between them. The Kenites were the descendants of Hobab, the father-in-law of Moses. They weren't Israelites, but they had long been friendly with the Israelites. They were related by marriage in the distant past.

When Sisera showed up at Jael's door, she graciously invited him in. That was also the custom. Nomadic people always extended gracious hospitality to those who came to their tents—it was considered a crime to turn someone away or to fail to offer that person whatever he might need in terms of food and water.

Sisera entered the tent and Jael covered him with a clean, dry blanket, and when he asked for some water, she went one better and opened a jug of milk and gave him a drink. She was a gracious hostess in every way. She fulfilled the law of hospitality.

Sisera felt so safe that he said, "Stand in the door of the tent, and let me know if anybody comes," and he went to sleep.

Then Jael remembered another law of the nomadic people— and that unwritten law stated that if a man found another man in the tent of his wife, he could kill his wife for being unfaithful. Jael wasn't about to let that happen!

She took a tent peg in one hand—a large nail-like spike of metal, about twelve inches long, used to secure the corner of a into the ground. She took a hammer in her other hand. As the wife of a nomadic man whose home was a tent, she knew how to handle a hammer and a tent spike. It was the responsibility of the women to raise and lower their own tents and pack them for travel from place to place. Jael was skilled at driving a tent spike into the ground.

She took this tent spike and hammer and walked softly up to the sleeping Sisera, drove that tent spike into his temples, and fastened his head to the ground. He never knew what hit him. He died right there, wrapped up in a blanket asleep in a woman's tent.

When Barak showed up at Jael's door, she went out to meet him and said, "Come, and I will show you the man you are looking for." When Barak went inside the tent, he found Sisera lying dead with a tent spike driven through his temples.

God's Word tells us, *"God subdued on that day Jabin the king of Canaan before the children of Israel. And the hand of the children of Israel prospered, and prevailed against Jabin the king of Canaan, until they had destroyed Jabin king of Canaan"* (Judg. 4:23–24).

The Israelites had rest for forty years after Sisera and Jabin were defeated. Once again, an entire generation knew what it meant to live in peace.

Are You Embracing Your Divine Destiny?

Time and time again I encounter people who claim to know God—claim to be saved, sanctified, and filled with the Holy Spirit—who will tell how God brought *them* into the world with a divine destiny, and yet they have no respect and no regard for the fact that God also brought *you* into this world with a divine destiny. Let me proclaim it to you loudly and clearly: God has a purpose for every creature, and He has a sovereign and eternal purpose for every person—including you.

God did not design a plan for you after you were born and grown up, and He saw who you were turning out to be. He had a plan designed for you even before your birth.

The Lord spoke these words through the prophet Isaiah:

- *Thus saith the LORD that made thee, and formed thee from the womb, which will help thee.* (Isa. 44:2)

- *Thus saith the LORD, thy redeemer, and he that formed thee from the womb, I am the LORD that maketh all things; that stretcheth forth the heavens alone; that spreadeth abroad the earth by myself.* (Isa. 44:24)

- *The LORD hath called me from the womb; from the bowels of my mother hath he made mention of my name.* (Isa. 49:1)

- *And now, saith the LORD that formed me from the womb to be his servant, to bring Jacob again to him, Though Israel be not gathered, yet shall I be glorious in the eyes of the LORD, and my God shall be my strength.* (Isa. 49:5)

Isaiah had no doubt that God, the Creator of all things, was his personal Creator. He did not doubt that the Lord had a purpose for his life before he was born, that God had destined him to be a servant of the Lord, and that what he did in fulfilling that destiny was pleasing to the Lord.

If you have any doubt today that God has called you with a divine call to be His, then you need to get that issue settled in your heart.

If you are willing to do whatever God calls you to do and to be the person God has created you to be, then there is only one person on this earth who can keep you from fulfilling your God-given destiny. That person is you.

God wants you to fulfill the purpose and plan for which He created you. He will move heaven and earth; He will defeat any enemy; He will come against any force that keeps you from that fulfillment. Only you, with an act of your will or an act of your negligence, can keep God's plan from being implemented. It's up to you to embrace God's plan for your life and then courageously set out to execute that plan.

Embrace His plan in your believing, your thinking, your feeling, your opinions, your attitude, your motivational level, and your entire inner being.

Execute His plan in your speaking, your doing, your relationship-building, your ministry, your actions, and your entire outer being.

When you do your part to be God's person and follow through on God's call, He will always do His part in being with you and working through you and using what you say and do to enact His greater eternal purposes. And He will always reward you with blessings, some now and a whole lot more in heaven.

On the other hand, if you refuse to heed His call or you refuse to seek out and fulfill your purpose, then God cannot use you or bless you as He desires.

The Lord once sent the prophet Jeremiah down to a potter's house so He could illustrate a great principle to him. Jeremiah *"went down to the potter's house, and, behold, he wrought a work on the wheels"* (Jer. 18:3)

I want you to notice that word *"wheels."* The Bible doesn't say *"wheel"*—rather, it says *"wheels."* There are two great wheels in which the Father molds and makes us. One is the wheel of time. He molds us and fashions us over time. Nobody is truly an instant success. Nobody is born with fully developed talents or skills. There is no such thing as overnight excellence.

God also uses the wheel of circumstance. He uses other people and situations to shape us and make us into vessels worthy of His use.

It is only as we yield to the Lord and remain faithful to Him over time and in all circumstances that the Lord can fully make us into the people He designed us to be.

You don't need to worry about liars, slanderers, jealous opponents, persecutors, or any other person who tries to keep you down or hold you back from fulfilling what you know is God's plan for you. God will take care of that person or that circumstance or that organization. Your role is to stay faithful and to continue to do what God has revealed to you to do. God's role is to be your defender, your shield, your strong tower, and your deliverer. Those people who come against you may just as well be battling the stars.

9

How Do You See Yourself: Victim or Person of Valor?

As a pastor, I have heard just about everything in counseling sessions. Some of the phrases I have heard a great deal are these:

"Well, my husband says I'm...."

"My wife thinks I'm...."

"People have always told me I'm...."

"I went to a psychologist who told me I'm...."

"A man prophesied over me one time that I'll be...."

"My friends all think I'm...."

I get to the point where I want to cry out, "What does God say about you?"

In the end, it doesn't matter what other people say about you.

It doesn't matter what the false prophets say about you...

It doesn't matter what the liars say about you...

It doesn't matter what the ungodly critics say about you…

It matters only what God says about you.

The same goes for circumstances.

Many people allow circumstances to dictate their behavior. They allow the situation they are in to define them or to determine their future. They allow the environment in which they were raised, or in which they find themselves, to define their character.

No! The only rightful definer of your life is God.

What God says is what matters.

A man named Gideon learned this in a dramatic way.

As you might expect, Gideon became a deliverer of the Israelites because *"the children of Israel did evil in the sight of the LORD"* (Judg. 6:1). This time, the Lord delivered them into the hand of the Midianites.

Who were these people?

The Midianites were a nomadic people who roamed from the Sinai Peninsula all the way to the banks of the Euphrates. They traded with people from Egypt to Lebanon. In some parts of the Bible, they are called the Ishmaelites. They are thought to be the descendants of Ishmael, the son of Abraham, born to Hagar, the Egyptian maid of Sarah.

The Midianites were the half-relatives of the Israelites. They both claimed Abraham as their distant relative. Like Ishmael, the Midianites were something of a wild people—they didn't have permanent homes or cities. They wandered from place to place, feeding off the pastures and crops of those they conquered in their path. They traded with this one and that, plundering whatever they could find and then selling it to whoever would buy. They eventually ceased to be an identifiable group, but rather, were absorbed into the Moabites and the Arabs in general.

In the days of Gideon, the Midianites operated like a roaming gang—and a very large gang at that. The Bible says their numbers were so great, and their cattle and camels so numerous, that they overran the Promised Land like a plague of grasshoppers.

The Bible says:

> And the hand of Midian prevailed against Israel: and because of the Midianites the children of Israel made them the dens which are in the mountains, and caves, and strong holds. And so it was, when Israel had sown, that the Midianites came up, and the Amalekites, and the children of the east, even they came up against them; and they encamped against them, and destroyed the increase of the earth, till thou come unto Gaza, and left no sustenance for Israel, neither sheep, nor ox, nor ass. For they came up with their cattle and their tents, and they came as grasshoppers for multitude; for both they and their camels were without number: and they entered into the land to destroy it. And Israel was greatly impoverished because of the Midianites; and the children of Israel cried unto the LORD.
> (Judg. 6:2–6)

The Midianites took over all the harvest of the fields for their own livestock and themselves, leaving nothing for the cattle, sheep, or oxen of the Israelites. The Israelites took to the caves in the hills and built for themselves *"dens"* in which to hide anything of value, including their lives, from plundering by the Midianites.

This was not the first or last time that the Israelites would take to the hills to hide out in the natural caves of the rugged mountains in the Promised Land. But it is the first time we read that a significant percentage of the population made their homes and hid themselves and whatever sustenance they had left in the dens, caves, and strongholds of the mountains.

The land was under siege for seven years before the children of Israel cried unto the Lord in confession and repentance. God's first response was not to send them deliverance, but a reminder—an explanation of sorts as to why they were under siege.

We read in God's Word:

And it came to pass, when the children of Israel cried unto the LORD because of the Midianites, that the LORD sent a prophet unto the children of Israel, which said unto them, Thus saith the LORD God of Israel, I brought you up from Egypt, and brought you forth out of the house of bondage; and I delivered you out of the hand of the Egyptians, and out of the hand of all that oppressed you, and drave them out from before you, and gave you their land; and I said unto you, I am the LORD your God; fear not the gods of the Amorites, in whose land ye dwell: but ye have not obeyed my voice. (Judg. 6:7–10)

God first sent a prophet saying, "This is why this has happened to you: You have not obeyed my voice." (See Judges 6:8–10.) There are times when we need to hear the prophets of the Lord who call us to repentance. Prophets don't only tell the future—they tell the truth about God's insistence on obedience and holiness among His people.

After sending the prophet, God sent an angel of the Lord to a man named Gideon.

And there came an angel of the LORD, and sat under an oak which was in Ophrah, that pertained unto Joash the Abiezrite: and his son Gideon threshed wheat by the winepress, to hide it from the Midianites. And the angel of the LORD appeared unto him, and said unto him, The LORD is with thee, thou mighty man of valour. And Gideon said unto him, Oh my Lord, if the LORD be with us, why then is all this befallen us? and where be all his miracles which our fathers told us of, saying, Did not the LORD bring us up from Egypt? but now the LORD hath forsaken us, and delivered us into the hands of the Midianites. And the LORD looked upon him, and said, Go in this thy might, and thou shalt save Israel from the hand of the Midianites: have not I sent thee? (Judg. 6:11–14)

Let me quickly remind you that every time the Israelites fell prey to an enemy, the reason was that the children of Israel *"did evil in the sight of the LORD."* Not only could the Israelites know this by reviewing their own history, but God also had sent a prophet with a direct word about why they were experiencing oppression from the Midianites. Even so, Gideon asked, "If the Lord is with us, then why have all these bad things happened to us?"

Gideon didn't realize how far he and the other Israelites had gone from the Lord. He made no connection between the evil the Israelites were doing and the bondage of the Midianites. And if he did, he believed God had sent the evil.

Many people in the world today draw the same erroneous conclusions. They see bad things as happening because of coincidence—being in the wrong place at the wrong time—or because another person is evil. Some blame God, calling Him a judgmental or punitive God who delights in causing pain and suffering.

People who do evil in the sight of the Lord rarely point the finger of blame for their oppression at themselves.

Now this is not to say that all bad things that happen to God's people are the result of sin. God's people aren't the only people in the world. There are ungodly people who are bent on doing evil. We live in a fallen world in which disease exists and accidents happen.

In a significant percentage of cases, however, the "bad" that has resulted in our lives is the result of our failing to love God and keep His commandments.

As a pastor, I am rarely called upon to counsel couples who are in a good marriage and only want it to be better. I don't think I've ever had a couple come to me and say, "Pastor, we have a wonderful marriage. Is there anything you can tell us that will make it even more wonderful?" What a joy it would be to do some of that kind of counseling!

Instead, I see couples who are on the brink of divorce. Things have gone terribly wrong in their marriage. As we begin to unravel the problems and get to the core issues, there's almost always a breach of God's commandments and God's judgments on the part of one, and usually both, of the spouses.

In many cases, those commandments and judgments were being broken even before the couple got married, but the couple didn't go for premarital counseling, which could have revealed that.

I once answered my phone to hear a woman say, "Pastor, you need to tell me what to do. This man I married beats me for breakfast, lunch, and dinner. He won't work. All he does is drink and swear and beat me up."

This same woman had told me not three months before, "Praise God, Pastor, I am marrying the man of my dreams. God has sent me a husband!"

The fact is, God didn't send that man to that woman. She decided she wanted him, and she married him.

The fact is, that man hadn't had a job for ten years. And not only that, but his father had never held down a steady job, and neither had his grandfather.

The fact is, that man had a reputation for drinking and getting angry and using his fists. Every person who regularly frequented a bar within a five-block area of their apartment knew that to be true.

But then came the clincher statement from this woman, "Oh, Pastor, why has God done this to me?"

This woman had no concept whatsoever that God had not had any part in doing anything to her. She had shut God out at the beginning of her relationship with this man—she hadn't consulted God about whether to date him, much less marry him. God had nothing to do with this man beating her up, drinking, swearing, or refusing to work. There was never any question about whether this man was going to go to church with his bride. He hadn't been in a church in decades, and he certainly wasn't going to be married in a church—they had eloped because, in her words, "we were just so much in love we couldn't wait to plan a big wedding."

It took a while for this woman to see that God had nothing to do with causing her pain. She had brought this bondage and suffering on herself.

People who are hurting don't want to think they've caused their own pain. It's much easier to blame somebody else, and if nobody else comes to mind, to blame God.

God never sent disaster upon the Israelites, either. Rather, He allowed enemies to conquer the land as a consequence of the evil that the Israelites did in His sight. When God withdrew, the enemies advanced. Any time God withdraws from a situation, evil rushes in. Any time good ceases, evil takes over. That's the law of action and consequence throughout the book of Judges and, indeed, the entire Bible.

In Gideon's case, you only have to read this story to see exactly the state of Gideon, his family, and the Israelites before God. Gideon's father had built a family altar to Baal. He had planted and cultivated a ceremonial grove of trees next to it as part of Baal worship. Gideon's family was worshipping Baal, and as the youngest son in that family, Gideon had no doubt been participating.

Gideon's family was among the poorest in the tribe. They weren't the rich and influential leaders of Manasseh—they were virtual nobodies in this tribe. You can be assured that if the poorest and least influential of the people had private altars and groves to Baal, then all the people of Manasseh likely had private altars and groves to Baal. Baal worship wasn't isolated here and there—it was throughout the land.

And so were the Midianites.

The abundance of Midianites that had swarmed into the Promised Land was mirrored by the abundance of altars and groves that had been built to Baal.

Gideon Saw Himself as a Victim

Gideon saw himself as a victim—not only of the Midianites, but also of God. When the angel of the Lord came to him, Gideon was threshing grain by the winepress. He was hiding out so he wouldn't be discovered. He had come out of his den or cave and down to the valley where he could thresh a little grain for his family, very likely under the cover of the night. He was threshing grain where grapes were normally pressed. Why do this? He was afraid of the Midianites.

When the angel of the Lord called him a mighty man of valor and told him to deliver the people from their oppression, Gideon replied that his family was the poorest family in Manasseh, and that he was the least in his father's house. He was saying to the angel of the Lord, "I'm a nobody and a nothing. Who am I to deliver Israel?" (See Judges 6:13–16.)

The Lord never takes your heritage as an excuse for failing to do what He calls you to do. In His eyes, it doesn't matter if you're black or white, tall or short, male or female, or any other attribute or feature of your physical, historical, material, or cultural life. What matters to the Lord is that He has a relationship with you. I'm God's child Papa I Love you

The angel of the Lord responded to Gideon, *"Surely I will be with thee, and thou shalt smite the Midianites as one man"* (Judg. 6:16).

"I will be with thee."

There aren't any more important words in the entire Bible.

There isn't any more important truth for your life.

How Do You See Yourself: Victim or Person of Valor?

[handwritten: my Papa]

God wants a relationship with you. *[handwritten: me]* He sent His Son to this earth to die on a cross so that He could free you from your sins and enter into a close fellowship with you. *[handwritten: me my Thank you my Jesus]*

God sent His Holy Spirit to dwell within you *[handwritten: me]* so that you would never again be separated from Him. He is with you always. *[handwritten: me]*

The fact is, Gideon most likely would have already died if God had not been with him. If he had been caught threshing grain in secret, the Midianites would have had no mercy.

[handwritten: No] Most of us can look back over our lives and draw the same conclusion—we are alive today because God has been with us. God has protected us to this moment because He still has something for us to do. *[handwritten: What do you want me to do]*

Gideon required even more evidence that the Lord was calling him to be a deliverer of his people. He wasn't even sure he was having a real conversation with a real entity. He thought he might be hallucinating or seeing and hearing things in the dark. He said, *"If now I have found grace in thy sight, then show me a sign that thou talkest with me."* He then said, *"Depart not hence, I pray thee, until I come unto thee, and bring forth my present, and set it before thee."* And the angel said, *"I will tarry until thou come again"* (Judg. 6:17–18).

Gideon slaughtered a kid and prepared it, made unleavened cakes with a little flour, put some of the meat in a basket and some broth in a pot, and he brought all this to the angel of the Lord and presented it to him. The angel said, "Take the flesh and the unleavened cakes, and lay them upon this rock, and pour out the broth." Gideon did as he was told. Then the angel of the Lord put forth the end of the staff that was in his hand, and he touched the meat and the unleavened cakes. Fire rose up from the rock and consumed the flesh and the unleavened cakes. And the angel of the Lord disappeared.

Gideon, at last, was convinced that he had experienced a real encounter with the Lord. He knew enough about the history of his

[handwritten: 3-10-24 Sunday 7:04 am]

own people to know that the fire was a divine sign of God's acceptance of an offering.

At that, he was even more afraid. The superstition of his day was that no person could have a face-to-face encounter with an angel of the Lord and continue to live. By the way, that was never something God said. Nevertheless, it was something Gideon believed.

Although the angel of the Lord had disappeared, the voice of the Lord remained, and the Lord said to Gideon, *"Peace be unto thee; fear not: thou shalt not die"* (Judg. 6:23).

Then God told Gideon to take a young bullock from his father's livestock, destroy the altar of Baal that his father had built, and cut down the ceremonial grove to Baal that was next to that altar. He told Gideon to build an altar unto the Lord upon the top of the rock from which the fire had come. Then He told Gideon to use the wood from the ceremonial grove and sacrifice the bull on the altar built to the Lord.

God called Gideon to action that would demonstrate faith.

God very often does the same in our lives. He calls us to act in obedience as a precondition of His acting in deliverance.

We say to God, "If You will act on my behalf, I'll quit my sin."

God says to us, "If you will obey My commandments and quit your sin, I'll act on your behalf."

I know a woman who says, "Lord, if You'll bless me, I'll quit shacking up with this man." God says, "Quit shacking up with that man so I can bless you!"

I know a man who says, "Lord, help me, and then I'll quit using these drugs." God says, "Quit using those drugs so I can help you!"

John the Baptist called to the people,

Bring forth therefore fruits meet for repentance: and think not to say within yourselves, We have Abraham to our father:

126

for I say unto you, that God is able of these stones to raise up children unto Abraham. And now also the axe is laid unto the root of the trees: therefore every tree which bringeth not forth good fruit is hewn down, and cast into the fire.

(Matt. 3:8–10)

It's not enough for you to say, "But I'm a saved, born-again Christian! I'm filled with the Holy Spirit!"

Now What God requires is that you live out the fruit of repentance. God requires that you bring forth pure, righteous, godly behavior out of your salvation and sanctification. *Do this*

Part of your living out the fruit of repentance is going to mean donning some spiritual armor to withstand what the devil never gives up trying to send your way.

Putting On Your Spiritual Armor

God calls each of us to put on our own spiritual armor. Nobody else can do this for us. God does not do this for us. It is something we are required to do. *ok*

The apostle Paul admonished the Ephesians to put on the whole armor of God so they could *"stand against the wiles of the devil"* (Eph. 6:11).

What are wiles? They are cunning devices. We need to be alert to the devil's tricks and temptations. Look at the verses that follow. The apostle Paul called for the believers to put on very specific pieces of armor that mean very specific things, to combat very specific wiles of the devil:

• *We Must Choose Truth instead of Giving In to Lying Enticements Associated with Sex. with sin*

Our loins are to be *"girt about with truth"* (Eph. 6:14). Lies associated with sex—our loins being the location of our sexual organs—are one of the devil's foremost temptations. We need to know God's truth about why He made us the way He did and what His purposes are for sex. We need to know how to behave sexually in a way that is pleasing to God. We need to know the truth of God's commandments about sexual behavior if we are going to be able to stand against the devil's temptations in this area of our lives. *Yes*

• *We Must Activate Our Will to Pursue Purity instead of Evil and Things Associated with the Occult.*

Our chest is to be protected with the *"breastplate of righteousness"* (Eph. 6:14). The chest is where the heart is located, which is Bible terminology for the will of man.

The Bible tells us that the heart of man is essentially wicked—we are drawn to evil, curious about the occult, quick to dabble in the dark arts. Even as children, we rush toward the scene of a fight or an accident, even though a small part of our subconscious is saying, "Don't go there. You might get hurt. Do you really want to see all that blood and gore?" This bent toward unrighteousness is to be replaced with a desire for righteousness. We must train our will to turn away from evil. If we are going to be delivered from evil, we must choose purity as an act of our will. *Not true*

We Are to Direct Our Steps toward Wholeness and Peace.

Few of us think of shoes as a part of armor, but think about how difficult it would be to fight a battle barefoot. God's Word says we are to have our feet *"shod with the preparation of the gospel of peace"* (Eph. 6:15). We are to be fully prepared at all times to move quickly into any situation to restore peace and wholeness. The Hebrew word for peace, *shalom,* also means healing and wholeness. We are to be agents of peace and healing.

Not only that, but we are to be *"shod,"* which means to wear sandals. In Bible times, slaves did not wear sandals. Only those who were the rightful heirs of a family had shoes. Only they were trusted to go out in the highways and markets to do business in the name of the family. God trusts us to have our shoes on as His rightful heirs, quick to conduct eternal spiritual business in His name.

• We Are to Have a Shield of Faith to Counteract Fear.

We are to cover our entire body with a *"shield of faith"* (Eph. 6:16). The shields of Paul's day were big and rectangular—like a door in shape and big enough to cover a man from his chin to his toes. Our entire life needs to be covered to *"quench all the fiery darts of the wicked"* (v. 16). What is the enemy of faith? The foremost enemy of faith is fear.

Take a look at the world around you and you'll see a world that is driven by fear. Fear of terrorism. Fear of failure. Fear of poverty. Fear of rejection. Fear of loss. Fear of never getting married or having children. Fear of disappointing someone you love. Fear of developing a dread disease. Fear of dying. The list is almost endless.

Little fears and big fears—they are fiery darts sent by the enemy. They are one of his cunning devices. If we are going to be delivered from this device of fear, we are going to have to develop our faith.

A number of years ago I heard a preacher define F-A-I-T-H as "For All, I Thank Him," "For All, I Trust Him," "For All, I Turn to Him." I like that definition! *Me too hallelujah!!*

• The Assurance of Our Salvation Protects Us against Doubt.

We are to don the *"helmet of salvation"* (Eph. 6:17). We are never to lose sight of the fact—calling it to our constant remembrance—that Christ died for us and we are, therefore, His possession and joint heirs with Him of all God's promises.

It is when we lose sight of all that Christ Jesus purchased for us on the cross that we begin to doubt. Doubt leads to discouragement. Discouragement leads to depression. Depression leads to despair.

The devil plants a little seed of doubt in our minds any time he can, saying, "You can't accomplish that good goal; you shouldn't say anything about Jesus now; you won't amount to anything; you aren't worthy to breathe the air in the room where you're sitting." Doubt is one of his wiles, his cunning devices to get us off track.

For many people, doubt is the biggest fiery dart the enemy has. Countless people who go to church every Sunday continue to doubt if God really exists. Others doubt if Jesus is the only way that a person can be saved.

A great deal is being taught today about black unity. I am proud of my color and my ethnicity. God made me who I am, and I accept His creation of me. But do not ask me to accept other people and become one with them solely because we share race or ethnicity. I cannot become one with a person who serves a different god than the one true and living God I serve. I cannot become unified with someone of another religion.

A great many blacks in our nation have turned to Islam because they have been told that Christianity is a white man's religion and was a religion foisted upon black people when they were slaves. The call made by Islam to blacks is that all blacks need to cast off the white man's religion, adopt Islam as a religion of their own, and become unified as a race. (I find it a bit ironic that Islam is the Arab man's religion first and foremost. It was no more the black man's religion in its origin than Christianity was the white man's religion—Christianity was originally the Jewish man's religion!)

Let me assure you of this—I'm not giving up Jesus for Muhammad. There's no comparison! If you want me to give up Jesus in order to be in unity with you, I'm never going to be in unity with you.

You've got to settle the issue of Jesus once and for all in your life. You need to determine with an absolute commitment that you are going to follow Christ no matter what happens to you.

You need to put doubt to rest.

If you truly want to be delivered, you must remind yourself continually that Christ died for you, and you are saved by His grace. Your hope of eternity lies in your relationship with Him as the Savior of your eternal soul. *my relationship is with my Jesus*

God's Word Is the Only Offensive Weapon We Need.

We are to take up the *"sword of the Spirit"* (Eph. 6:17). It is by the Word that we defeat the devil. Jesus used the Word in His confrontation with the devil, who came to tempt Him after His baptism. He used only a few verses from the Old Testament to cause the devil to flee from Him. Just think—He's given us thousands of verses in the Bible to choose from in defeating the devil today!

The devil will do whatever he can to keep you from hearing, reading, or studying God's Word. He'll tell you that you don't have time to read your Bible daily; you shouldn't listen to that preacher for one reason or another; you shouldn't spend Sunday mornings and Sunday evenings and Wednesday evenings in church; you don't have time to go to that Bible study or the money to go on that Bible-centered spiritual retreat. Ignorance about what God's Word *note* says and means is a major weapon of the enemy against us. Spiritual ignorance is one of the devil's favorite wiles. If you truly want to be delivered, you need to take the responsibility of reading and studying the Bible for yourself.

And oh, the darts do fly!

One dart flies at you from one direction.

Another comes at you from another direction.

At times, you get hit!

But God's promise to those who take on these six pieces of spiritual armor is that they will be able to *"withstand in the evil day"* (Eph. 6:13).

halleluah ! . Jesus

Scud Missiles instead of Fiery Darts

If the apostle Paul was living in today's world, he may very well have likened the weapons of the enemy to Scud missiles or rockets with homing devices. Just as the enemies of the Israelites had a new, more advanced technology in the time of the judges, so the enemy uses the technological advancements of today to couch his temptations.

Always be aware that the enemy launches his darts using the latest and finest in technology and possessions. Now that isn't to say we can't use and be blessed by technology and possessions. Just be aware that the devil will come at you in the guise of things that are the latest fad, the newest innovation, or the most modern invention. In instances too numerous to recount, the enemy seems to have led the way in an evil use of technology before godly people could figure out how to harness a technology for good. Just as the enemies of the Israelites came to them with iron chariots and spears, so the enemy today comes at you with the newest "in" method or object.

One of his most powerful launch-pads is the media—from radio to television, computers to movies, and billboards to magazines and books.

The lure of lust has been made only more potent by today's technology.

The lust for things—the grip of greed—is made more potent by all the images we see daily of things we are told we should have and could have if we will only compromise in the way the devil desires for us to compromise our values and our character.

The lust for power is made stronger by today's technology. We can see the kingdoms of this world on nightly television, with a heavy dose of sex worked into the TV movie on the cable channel, and a heavy dose of materialism worked into the commercials.

We are tempted.

My Jesus Says I Am

We are enticed.

We are trapped.

And in the face of it all, God declares, "I am your Lord. I am the way, the truth, and the life. I am your Sovereign and Supreme Judge. Look to Me, trust Me, worship Me, follow Me. Be My person in the midst of your enemies, and I will give you total freedom in your Land of Promise!"

Oh, may it be so in your life and mine! *It is So*

Note Gideon Built an Altar to God

The good news in the life of Gideon is that he chose to obey the voice of God and to do what God commanded him to do. He got ten men who were servants of his family to help him, and he did exactly as the Lord had said—only at night because he was afraid to do all this in the light of day. He knew the men of the city would be angry when they saw what had happened, and he was right.

The leaders of that area quickly determined that Gideon was the one who had cut down the trees and destroyed the altar to Baal, and they told Joash, *"Bring out thy son, that he may die: because he hath cast down the altar of Baal, and because he hath cut down the grove that was by it"* (Judg. 6:30). Joash refused—he said, in essence, "Let Baal deal with him. If Baal is upset, let Baal exact vengeance." Joash asked the men, "Will you plead for Baal? Those who plead for Baal should be the ones put to death!"

Joash wasn't upset at what his son had done—Gideon's actions had brought Joash to his senses.

What will it take for you to be brought to your senses? What will it take for God to get through to you that He requires your obedience to His commandments and your wholehearted love? What will it take for God to convince you that He is a jealous God and He refuses to share your affection and devotion with any false god or idol?

It was after Gideon had torn down the altar and grove to Baal and had built an altar and made a sacrifice on it to God—a tremendous sign of repentance and turning back to the Lord as the one, true, and living God—that the Spirit of the Lord came upon Gideon. (See Judges 6:34.)

When the Spirit of the Lord came upon him, Gideon blew a trumpet and rallied others to God's cause—first his family, then people from throughout Manasseh his tribe, and then men from the tribes of Asher, Zebulun, and Naphtali.

Meanwhile, the Midianites had joined with the Amalekites and the *"children of the east"* and had moved into the great valley of Jezreel.

Everything was set for a showdown.

10

Learning to Use God's Methods

God not only tells His people what to do, but through the leading of the Holy Spirit, He also tells them specifically when to act, how to act, where to go, the words to speak, and the actions to take. Never doubt that God has a thoroughly detailed plan for your deliverance and for your ongoing possession and occupying of the place He has for you. God sees every aspect of every situation, knows every facet of every personality, and counts every minute of every day. He knows the methods He has prepared for you.

When Gideon sounded the trumpet, thirty-two thousand men rallied to his side by the well of Harod, which was south of the area where a very large contingent of Midianites was camped.

Gideon again needed reassurance. He asked God to give him a sign that He truly was going to save Israel through him. He put a fleece of wool on the ground and said to the Lord, *"If the dew be on the fleece only, and it be dry upon all the earth beside, then shall I know that thou wilt save Israel by mine hand, as thou hast said"* (Judg. 6:37). And it happened just that way. The next morning there was so much dew on that fleece that Gideon was able to wring a bowl-full of water from it, but all the ground around it was dry.

Gideon asked a second time, *"Let not thine anger be hot against me, and I will speak but this once: let me prove, I pray thee, but this once with the fleece; let it now be dry only upon the fleece, and upon all the ground let there be dew"* (v. 39). And the next morning, the fleece was bone dry, but there was dew on all the ground around it. (See Judges 6:36–40.)

Some people have criticized Gideon for putting God to a test, but I don't criticize him for that. For at least the last seven years, and perhaps for long before that, Gideon had not heard the Word of the Lord spoken into his life. No one around him had been talking about the commandments of the Lord. No prophet among the Israelites had been proclaiming the Word of the Lord. No one among his family or friends had been recounting the miracles or the judgments of God. Gideon had experienced a supernatural encounter with an angel of the Lord down by a winepress in the dark one night. He had heard God's voice commanding him to tear down an altar and grove to Baal and build an altar to the Lord.

Now, a multitude of Midianites, Amalekites, and people from the east have set up camp in the great valley of Jezreel. People from Asher, Zebulun, and Naphtali, as well as members of his own tribe of Manasseh, have rallied to his side. A battle is about to take place.

Gideon—the least of his father's sons and his family the poorest in Manasseh—was at the center of it all. People were looking to him for leadership. And Gideon had every reason to be both fearful and very much in need of making certain that he had heard God accurately.

Gideon didn't go to the Lord to challenge, test, or provoke the Lord. He went seeking confirmation that what he had heard from the angel of the Lord was still in effect.

God never faults us for asking confirmation of His word to us. In fact, the Lord said in the law that, for Israelites, truth would be established among them out of the mouth of two witnesses. The great prophets of the Lord never spoke anything that was in disagreement with the law given to Moses. The spoken, Holy Spirit-inspired word of God always matched up with the written Word of God.

Trust God to Confirm His Word

If you have questions today about whether something you have been thinking about or something you have heard in your spirit or seen in a vision is from God, ask God to confirm that message to you. Go to your Bible and seek out evidence that what you have heard is in keeping with the cover-to-cover truth of God's Word. Don't just look for one little verse or phrase to support your case or your belief. Take the whole of God's Word as your standard of evaluation. Do you see examples in which God has said a similar thing to other people? Do you see examples in which God has called other people to a similar mission? Do you see examples in which God has honored and rewarded with blessing the behavior that He is calling you to manifest?

We get in trouble on this when we go to this person or that person and say, "What do you think of this message I received from the Lord?" Their opinion is only as good as their relationship with the Lord. If the person you ask is a true man or woman of God, a person who knows their Bible from cover to cover, then you may be on solid ground in seeking his or her opinion—but always listen closely to see if that person references the Word of God in responding to you or if that person responds solely out of his or her experience or emotions. God's Word confirms God's word.

Gideon didn't have God's Word to consult. He was looking for two witnesses directly from God to confirm the truth of God's message to him. And God gave him what he needed.

Do you need to put out a fleece today? No. God has given you His Word to read and study.

Will God answer you if you ask Him to guide your reading and studying so you can get a clear answer to your question or to feel confirmation in your spirit? I have no doubt He will.

God wants you to know with precision and accuracy what it is that He has created you to be, called you to say, and challenged you to do. He doesn't expect you to go groping about in the dark of ignorance, hoping you'll stumble upon His will. He wants you to know with certainty who you are in Christ Jesus, how you are to live in this world, and what you are to do to be the best witness you can be for the Gospel's sake.

①   • God will answer the questions you have.

②.   • God will show you the path to take.

③.   • God will reveal to you the timing and methods He wants you to use.

④.   God will lead you to the people who are to be involved with you or be in relationship with you.

⑤.   • God will resolve the problems that arise along the path of your obedience.

There are far more problems experienced by saints of God who fail to ask God to confirm His word than there are problems experienced by those who ask for confirmation with a humble heart.

Once Gideon had confirmation from the Lord, he began to act. He never put out another fleece.

Note →   We need to take wisdom from this as well. Learn to hear God's voice. Get on the same frequency. Tune Him in. And once you know God's voice, don't keep second-guessing what He says to you. Get yourself prepared for action. Ask God how He intends for you to proceed.

Specific Directions for How to Proceed

The Lord spoke to Gideon and said:

The people that are with thee are too many for me to give the Midianites into their hands, lest Israel vaunt themselves against me, saying, Mine own hand hath saved me. Now therefore go to, proclaim in the ears of the people, saying, Whosoever is fearful and afraid, let him return and depart early from mount Gilead. (Judg. 7:2–3)

There's some humor in this. Can you see it? Here is Gideon, a man who was so fearful that he was threshing a little grain by a winepress at night because he was afraid of the Midianites, now saying to others, "Those of you who are afraid may go home."

Twenty-two thousand of the thirty-two thousand left. Two out of three men were willing to say, "I'm scared. I'm leaving."

The Lord said to Gideon, *"The people are yet too many; bring them down unto the water, and I will try them for thee there: and it shall be, that of whom I say unto thee, This shall go with thee, the same shall go with thee; and of whomsoever I say unto thee, This shall not go with thee, the same shall not go"* (Judg. 7:4).

Gideon brought the people to the spring, and there, the Lord said to Gideon, *"Every one that lappeth of the water with his tongue, as a dog lappeth, him shalt thou set by himself; likewise every one that boweth down upon his knees to drink"* (Judg. 7:5).

Three hundred men put their hand to their mouth. The rest of the ten thousand bowed down upon their knees to drink water directly from the spring.

The Lord said to Gideon, *"By the three hundred men that lapped will I save you, and deliver the Midianites into thine hand:*

and let all the other people go every man unto his place" (Judg. 7:7).

Nine thousand seven hundred men went home.

Gideon saw thirty-one thousand seven hundred people walk away from him and away from the battle at the Lord's command. He was left standing with three hundred.

God said, "Tonight's the night." And, knowing Gideon's heart, God then said to him, *"If thou fear to go down, go thou with Phurah thy servant down to the host* [of the Midianites]: *and thou shalt hear what they say; and afterward shall thine hands be strengthened to go down unto the host"* (Judg. 7:10–11).

Gideon took Phurah and they went to the edge of the camp of the armed soldiers. There, hiding in the shadows, they heard a man tell a dream to a fellow soldier. He said, *"Behold, I dreamed a dream, and, lo, a cake of barley bread tumbled into the host of Midian, and came unto a tent, and smote it that it fell, and overturned it, that the tent lay along"* (v. 13).

The man who heard this dream said, *"This is nothing else save the sword of Gideon the son of Joash, a man of Israel: for into his hand hath God delivered Midian, and all the host"* (v. 14).

When Gideon heard this dream and the interpretation given to it, he worshipped God and returned to the host of Israel and said, *"Arise; for the Lord hath delivered into your hand the host of Midian"* (v. 15).

God again confirmed to Gideon the truth of His word that God was going to deliver the Israelites through Gideon and those who had rallied to him.

Gideon divided the three hundred men into three companies. He put a trumpet in every man's hand, and for the other hand, he gave them an empty pitcher with a lamp in it. He said,

> *Look on me, and do likewise: and, behold, when I come to the outside of the camp, it shall be that, as I do, so shall ye*

do. When I blow with a trumpet, I and all that are with me,
then blow ye the trumpets also on every side of all the camp,
and say, The sword of the Lord, and of Gideon.

(Judg. 7:17–18)

The three companies of one hundred Israelites each fanned out around the perimeter of the camp of the Midianites, up in the foothills. They blew their trumpets, broke their pitchers to expose the lamps in them, and when the people in the valley heard the trumpets, saw the lights, and heard the shouts of people crying, *"The sword of the Lord, and of Gideon,"* they ran, cried, and fled in the darkness. They began to fight one another, not recognizing their allies as Midianite, Amalekite, or people of the east in the confusion of the night.

As these armies killed one another and began to flee, the men of Israel in Naphtali and Asher and the rest of Manasseh pursued those who were fleeing. They drove the Midianites to the waters of Bethbarah and the Jordan, and there, the men of Ephraim came to the battle and took control over the waterways. The main princes of the Midianites, Oreb and Zeeb, were killed.

Gideon and his forces pursued the Midianites across the Jordan, and there he killed two more prominent kings of Midian, Zebah and Zalmunna, as well as the remaining host of about fifteen thousand soldiers in the Midianite army. In all, more than a hundred and twenty thousand soldiers—Midianites, Amalekites, and *"children of the east"*—died at the hands of Gideon and the Israelites under his command. The Bible says, *"Thus was Midian subdued before the children of Israel, so that they lifted up their heads no more"* (Judg. 8:28). In other words, they no longer considered themselves a formidable force capable of warring against or oppressing the Israelites.

The Israelites enjoyed *"quietness"* (Judg. 8:28) for forty years after this great victory. For his part, Gideon returned to his home city of Ophrah. He *"dwelt in his own house"* (v. 29) and had many wives—who produced seventy sons. The Bible tells us that Gideon *"died in a good old age"* (Judg. 8:32).

God's Plan for Your "Quietness"

When people say to me that they are going to retire, my first question is, "And do what?"

The only reason to retire from something God has called you to do is to do something else God has called you to do.

Most people I know fail to ask God for His directions and plan after they are delivered. They trust God for a mighty breakthrough, a powerful deliverance, a miraculous turnaround. But then they don't ask God to reveal to them how they are to live once they have been delivered, healed, restored, reconciled, or brought to safety.

There's no mention of Gideon ever having to defend anybody in Israel again. The people served God and obeyed God and an entire generation knew what it meant to live in the Promised Land in peace.

Nevertheless, there was one small stumbling block. The people of Israel had said to Gideon, *"Rule thou over us, both thou, and thy son, and thy son's son also: for thou hast delivered us from the hand of Midian"* (Judg. 8:22). They wanted Gideon to be their king. Gideon refused. He wisely understood that God had not called him to be a king—only a deliverer from the Midianites.

Gideon said to them, *"I will not rule over you, neither shall my son rule over you: the Lord shall rule over you"* (v. 23).

But Gideon made a request of them. He asked the men of Israel to turn over to him the earrings of the soldiers who had died. The Ishmaelites had a custom of wearing golden earrings, so Gideon knew that in taking the spoil of the enemy, the people had amassed thousands of gold earrings. The men of Israel willingly gave these to Gideon, along with other ornaments, crescents and chains from the Ishmaelite camels, and the purple raiment from the kings. The weight of the gold was about fifty-seven pounds!

Gideon made an ephod from this offering—a holy ornamental breastplate that was similar to the ones the priest had worn in the tabernacle—and he put that ephod in his city of Ophrah. It no doubt was a symbol to Gideon that the battle had been the Lord's and that the Lord was the only One worthy to be worshipped and praised in all of Israel. The ephod was a symbol of the people living in total submission and obedience to the Lord. It was a symbol that the people belonged to God, and God alone was worthy of their love.

Over time, however, the people went *"a whoring after"* (v. 27) this ephod. That means they began to worship the ephod more than they worshipped God. They started worshipping the physical symbol rather than the substance of the invisible God.

Some people do this today. They move from worshipping God to worshipping the symbols they have associated with God. They worship their church—the building, the stained glass windows, the beautiful interior, the steeple, the bell tower. They worship their liturgy—their rituals and the traditions they have, their method or manner of singing and speaking and holding special services. They substitute the trappings of their faith for the real substance of God's holiness in their midst.

God wants us to worship Him in spirit and in truth—with nothing standing in the way.

Nothing must become a substitute for His presence.

Nothing must become a substitute for His glory.

We must never allow ourselves to see anything as being necessary for our approach to God other than a humble, repentant heart.

The ephod of Gideon became a snare to Gideon and his house. What Gideon had thought was a good thing became something that tripped up his family.

Let me repeat—God had not told Gideon to take up the gold earrings of the fallen Ishmaelites. He had not told Gideon to make this ephod. This was Gideon's idea.

Be aware, and beware! After God has delivered you from an enemy, you are likely going to want to do something to show your thanksgiving and praise to God. You may want to build a monument to the victory God has given you. You may want to do something as a display to others that God is the One who saved you, healed you, delivered you, and blessed you.

Your heart and your motivation may be right. But don't do anything unless God tells you specifically what to do.

God is not only the Source of your deliverance, but He also desires to be the One who directs your response to His deliverance.

The lord told me this morning to plant a seed. A thought in
my mind a seed of my heart my mind and the holy spirit
said Kindness love mercy ✓ then pray praise & thank
God I also Bind the enemy of

II

---•◦❦◦•---

Stay Where the Lord Is Most Likely to Show Up!

A re all negative circumstances or situations linked to personal sin?

No.

Do we sometimes find ourselves in enemy territory or in dire need through no sinful behavior on our part?

Yes.

Not all tragedy, sickness, or trouble is the direct result of our personal turning to false gods or engaging in the worship of idols. The truth is, we live in a fallen world—we live in the environment of a fallen creation and among people who are fallen people. We live in a world in which the devil has been allowed a degree of freedom to persecute God's people.

When I was a boy, people talked about being scared of the "greaser man." This man supposedly wore no clothes—he just greased his body heavily. And when you tried to capture that man or hold on to him, he always slipped away because he was so greasy. You couldn't get anything on the greaser man, and you couldn't get back anything he took from you.

The devil works against us like the greaser man. He never stays around for you to pin anything on him—and he doesn't give back what he steals from you. Only the Lord Jesus Christ can grab hold of the greasy ol' devil and force him to give back to you what he has taken from you.

We also live in a world in which sinful acts abound in the lives of people all around us. We are not immune from the crimes these sinful people commit, the evil they perpetrate, or the wickedness they spread through a community.

The fault or failure may not be ours personally—we may have nothing to do with the worship of false gods; we may not be in disobedience to God's commandments—but we are nevertheless part of a greater whole that is pursuing sin, not righteousness.

Don't ever lay a guilt trip on a person, saying that his cancer or other dread disease is the result of his personal sin. It may or may not be related to personal sin. It may be that the person simply lives in a world in which cancer is one aspect of the fallen creation.

Don't ever lay upon a person the blame that his business was burned by an arsonist, or his home was robbed and ransacked, or his child was kidnapped because of his personal sin. It may or may not be related to personal sin. It may be that the family or person simply lives in a world in which evil people commit evil acts against the innocent.

In the *"days when the judges ruled"* a great famine arose in the land of the Israelites. The story that is told in that context is one of the most famous stories in the Bible—it is the story of Ruth. It is the story of a family that did not appear to worship false gods or live in disobedience. They, nevertheless, were victims of a great famine.

Stay Where the Lord Is Most Likely to Show Up!

Such a famine is described in the book of Judges. The Midianites, Amalekites, and the children of the east came in massive numbers to steal the crops and flocks, leaving no sustenance for the Israelites. The Bible says, *"Israel was greatly impoverished because of the Midianites"* (Judg. 6:6). This famine was the result of an invasion—it was not a natural famine coming from the lack of rain. Nevertheless, it was a famine, and the consequences were severe and prolonged. It lasted seven years.

What Do You Do in Times of Famine?

A man named Elimelech from Bethlehemjudah (the place we know as Bethlehem today) couldn't wait out the famine. He and his family were starving and in need, so this man went in search of food and a life without severe oppression. He left the Promised Land to dwell in Moab along with his wife, Naomi, and his two sons named Mahlon and Chilion. They were descendants of Ephratha, one of the wives of Caleb, so they were of a prominent family in a well-known place in the Promised Land.

Even so, they were victims of the famine. That happens today. Tragedy can and does strike even the best of families, including the best of families with a long heritage of loving and serving the Lord.

Was Elimelech right in leaving Bethlehem for Moab? No, I don't believe he was. I believe he was on the verge of experiencing God's deliverance, but he didn't have the patience or perseverance to see the victory that God was sending. This man was living in Bethlehem, which literally means the "house of bread," in the tribe of Judah, which means "praise." He left the place of sustenance and praise for a home in what God called an enemy land.

Although I don't believe Elimelech was right in leaving, I can understand from a human standpoint why he left. The people all around him were doing evil in the sight of the Lord. His family was starving, and his sons apparently weren't very strong or healthy—the

Mahlon

Chilion

name of one of them means "sick" and the name of the other means "pining" or "wasting away." Elimelech no doubt saw things in Moab as being no less evil than in the land where he was dwelling.

On that point, he was wrong. Of all the places he should not have gone in search of food, he should not have gone to Moab. The Moabites had been totally rejected by God, and the commandment to the Israelites was not to accept the Moabites or have any fellowship with them. Moab was not the place God wanted Elimelech to be.

If the community in which you live has no jobs, you might need to move to a community in which you can work and support your family. But don't turn to dealing drugs or stealing cars to put bread on the table!

If the church you attend doesn't have an opportunity for you to sing, you may be led by God to a church with a choir. But don't turn to singing in nightclubs!

And if you move from that community or that church, make sure that God is leading you away to a new place of provision and service. Don't leave mad at folks you believe have rejected you or with an attitude of revenge. Don't leave a place of employment angry and vengeful because your company had to cut back its workforce or moved its operations elsewhere. Go in peace to serve the Lord—don't leave in bitterness to serve the devil.

Things may get tight where you are, but that doesn't mean the place where God has you is wrong. It may be the place is tight but right!

Jesus never promised any one a life that didn't have some tight spots or some tragedy. He told a story in which He said:

> *Whosoever heareth these sayings of mine, and doeth them, I will liken him unto a wise man, which built his house upon a rock: and the rain descended, and the floods came, and the*

Wow Papa God - you are straight forward

winds blew, and beat upon that house; and it fell not: for it was founded upon a rock. And every one that heareth these sayings of mine, and doeth them not, shall be likened unto a foolish man, which built his house upon the sand: and the rain descended, and the floods came, and the winds blew, and beat upon that house; and it fell: and great was the fall of it.
(Matt. 7:24–27)

Notice that the rain descended and the floods came and the winds blew on both the wise and the foolish. Being wise, or being in relationship with the Lord Jesus Christ, doesn't immunize a person from fierce storms that are marked by floods and damaging winds. The call of God is to be faithful and wise in the midst of a tight time. God tells us in His Word that those who persevere in a time of trouble are those who are saved from that trouble. (See Mark 13:13.)

Don't Be Quick to Leave

Don't be quick to leave when famine strikes you—no matter what the nature of that famine is. It may be a famine of provision, a famine of health, or a famine of love. Don't be quick to run away. Go only if God leads you out to a specific place He has prepared for you and called you to.

Don't Be Led by Life's "Ifs"

Our world operates on a lot of "if" principles:

- "If it feels good, do it."

- "If it seems right, pursue it."

- "If it has the potential for a good ending, go for it."

There are hundreds of thousands of people in our nation who thought something felt good, but they are dying today as a result of those good feelings. There are millions who did what seemed right to them personally at the time, but they are suffering today because what was right to them was wrong before God. There are countless people who thought an end justified the means, but they are hung up in the means today and have no hope of seeing a good end.

Felt-good, seemed-right-to-me, justified-by-what-seemed-to-be-a-good-end behavior has caused untold numbers of people to suffer and die from AIDS, the divorce rate in our nation to be nearly one out of two, the number of abused children and spouses to sky-rocket, the abortion rate to top 30 million babies, and the level of despair and discouragement to rise like flood waters.

Note this

Don't Go Where Jesus Isn't

Yes

Choose to remain at the center of a place where Jesus is welcomed and proclaimed as Savior and Lord. Choose to remain in places where the Holy Spirit is allowed to do His work and bestow His gifts. Stay where Jesus is lifted up and His name is praised.

The disciples of Jesus experienced something of a famine time in their personal ministry. Jesus had gone to the top of a high mountain with Peter, James, and John. The other nine disciples continued to engage in ministry at the foot of the mountain. A man brought his son to them for healing and deliverance, but the disciples were unable to help him. The boy suffered from what the Bible calls a *"dumb spirit"*—it was a demonic spirit that tore away at his body, causing him to foam at the mouth and gnash his teeth. At times the demon sought to destroy the boy by throwing him into a fire, and at other times, into water. The disciples did all they could do, but the boy was not delivered.

But then, Jesus came down from the mountain, and He came down to His disciples.

Don't leave the church for the local bar. Jesus isn't going to show up there.

Don't leave the church to hang out on the local street corner. Jesus isn't going to show up there.

Jesus is going to show up where His disciples are!

When Jesus showed up on this scene, He rebuked that foul spirit in that boy, saying, *"Thou dumb and deaf spirit, I charge thee, come out of him, and enter no more into him"* and immediately the spirit cried and seemed to rip him in two—but it came out. The boy was delivered completely. (See Mark 9:14–29.)

You may be in a church right now where you don't see any miracles. You may be praying and casting out demons without seeing any result. You may be praying without receiving any answers. Your preacher may be preaching without any souls being saved.

It may be famine time in your church or in your personal ministry or in your devotional time with the Lord. God may seem to be absent from your midst!

But let me assure you, if you will hold fast and continue to do what you know to do—fasting and praying and searching God's Word and trusting in faith—Jesus is going to come down from the top of the mountain and bring you the deliverance you need. *Halleluah Jesus*

God does not call people to dwell in the house of bread and then fail to give them bread when they call out to Him! God does not call people to dwell in the tribe of praise and then fail to respond to their praise.

Keep praising the Lord. *Yes*

Keep trusting the Lord. *Yes*

Keep calling out to the Lord. *Yes*

He'll come to you! *Halleluah*

There is no mention that Elimelech was following the leading of the Lord in going to Moab. There is no mention that Elimelech praised God, called out to God, or trusted God to provide for his family regardless of the famine all around him. No, all indications are that Elimelech was operating strictly on his own reasoning in leaving Bethlehem for Moab. And as it turned out, within ten years, this man died in Moab, along with his two sons. The place Elimelech thought was a place of provision turned out to be a place of death.

In the ten years that Elimelech's family lived in Moab, however, the sons married two Moabite girls—one named Orpah, the other Ruth. After the death of her husband and sons, Naomi found herself a widow without heirs, but with two daughters-in-law. Her future in Moab was even bleaker than her future had been in Bethlehem.

Returning to the House of Bread

Naomi heard that God had once again provided bread in the house of bread. She made plans to return home. She blessed her two daughters-in-law, saying, *"Go, return each to her mother's house: the Lord deal kindly with you, as ye have dealt with the dead, and with me. The Lord grant you that ye may find rest, each of you in the house of her husband."* Then she kissed the girls in blessing (Ruth 1:8–9).

One of the girls, Orpah, went back home. Ruth said to her mother-in-law,

> *Entreat me not to leave thee, or to return from following after thee: for whither thou goest, I will go; and where thou lodgest, I will lodge: thy people shall be my people, and thy God my God: where thou diest, will I die, and there will I be buried: the Lord do so to me, and more also, if ought but death part thee and me.* (Ruth 1:16–17)

There was something about Naomi's Lord that had an irresistible appeal to Ruth. She wanted the God of the Israelites.

She returned with Naomi, and as the story turns out, Ruth met a relative of Elimelech. This man, named Boaz, married Ruth and they had a son they named Obed. He, in turn, had a son named Jesse. He, in turn, had a son named David.

Ruth became the great-ancestor of Jesus, who was born of the line of King David!

Stay Where the Lord Is Most Likely to Show Up!

God completely reversed the error of Elimelech. He restored Naomi fully to her people. He caused good to come out of a bad decision.

Trust God to do that in your life.

You may have made a bad decision. You may have erred. You may have sinned. You may be in a bad situation as a result.

But don't quit now.

Don't close the book now.

Don't end the story.

Let God write another chapter! *Amen thank for Jesus*

I'm not saying that it's good your spouse walked out on you or that your divorce is good, but I know this—God isn't through with you yet.

I'm not saying that the death of a loved one is good, but I know this—God has miracles He hasn't performed yet.

I'm not saying that the loss of your job is good, but I know this—God is capable of providing for you every day, in every way.

What started out in famine ended up in abundant blessing for Naomi. And what God did then, God does now. *Yes Papa God*

God can turn around your situation, no matter how bad it may be. *Yes thank for Jesus*

God can provide bread for you, even when a famine has engulfed you. *Halleluah*

God can provide an inheritance for you, even when it seems the devil has destroyed your inheritance. *Jesus my deliver*

God can open a new door. *J claim that God will in my life.*

He can provide a new method, means, or way. *Yes Amen*

He can raise you to a new height. *J except*

Trust Him to do it. *Papa God you are doing your will in my life Right Now*

3-1-2024 8.06pm Monday

153

12

Don't Put Up with Misery

H ave you ever met a person who thought it was just his or her lot in life to suffer?

Have you ever met a person who sighs in the face of terrible circumstances and says, "Well, that's just the way it is"?

God has never called upon His people to sit idly by and put up with misery. He calls us to engage in spiritual warfare, lift our praises to God, be victorious over the enemy of our lives, and win battles in the name of the Lord.

Misery comes to us in many forms. We need to be aware of them so we can fight against them. One of the forms misery takes is the sending of a miserable person into our midst.

That's what happened to the Israelites after Gideon died.

A Miserable Man Who Was a Wanna-Be King

One would think that the victory won by the Lord through Gideon was so great that nobody would ever want to turn away from the Lord. That wasn't the case.

The Bible tells us,

As soon as Gideon was dead, that the children of Israel turned again, and went a whoring after Baalim, and made Baalberith their god. And the children of Israel remembered not the LORD their God, who had delivered them out of the hands of all their enemies on every side: neither showed they kindness to the house of Jerubbaal, namely, Gideon, according to all the goodness which he had showed unto Israel.
(Judg. 8:33–35)

Now Gideon had seventy sons by many wives. Let that thought sink in. He had yet another son by a concubine, not a wife, who lived in Shechem.

This son born to the concubine, Abimelech, took money from the temple of Baalberith and hired men to follow him, and they killed all of the sons of Gideon except one. Sixty-nine of Gideon's seventy sons died. Only Jotham escaped, but not before he cursed Abimelech and the men of Shechem who proclaimed Abimelech to be their king.

Jotham told a parable that pointed out to the men of Shechem how ridiculous it was for them to choose a misery-causing man like Abimelech to be their king. He said:

The trees went forth on a time to anoint a king over them; and they said unto the olive tree, Reign thou over us. But the olive tree said unto them, Should I leave my fatness, wherewith by me they honour God and man, and go to be promoted over the trees? And the trees said to the fig tree, Come thou, and reign over us. But the fig tree said unto them, Should I forsake my sweetness, and my good fruit, and go to be promoted over the trees? Then said the trees unto the vine, Come thou, and reign over us. And the vine said unto them, Should I leave my wine, which cheereth God and man, and go to be promoted over the trees? Then said all the trees unto the bramble, Come thou, and reign over us. And the bramble said unto the trees, If in truth ye anoint me king over you, then come and put your trust in my shadow:

155

and if not, let fire come out of the bramble, and devour the
cedars of Lebanon. (Judg. 9:8–15)

Abimelech was a worthless man—he had no integrity, no valor, no character that produces good fruit. He was a bramble, which is the same as saying a thistle or a tumbleweed.

Abimelech was not only a half-breed in his physical heritage, but he was also a half-breed spiritually. He wanted the power and position that Gideon and his rightful heirs knew better than to desire!

The trouble with following worthless people is that they eventually bring you to destruction. Not only do they have no good fruitfulness in their own lives, but they destroy your fruitfulness. They cause you misery.

- If you join hands with murderers, one day they will murder you.

- If you join your heart to gossipers, one day the gossip will be about you.

- If you link up with thieves, one day they will steal from you.

- If you associate with liars, one day their lies will be about you.

Be wary of those who seek fame and power for themselves. They are not people God blesses with His fullness. God blesses people who give Him glory and honor.

Indeed, Abimelech ruled as king for three years, and then he was killed by a woman who cast a millstone from a tower and broke his skull. The men of Shechem who had made Abimelech their king were killed in a fire at the temple of the false god Berith. It was an ugly, horrible period in Israel's history. All that Abimelech had done to the sons of Gideon was done to him, and all that Jotham had prophesied against the men of Shechem came to pass.

After Abimelech's brief reign as king, God raised up a judge named Tola, an Ephraimite, to judge Israel. He judged Israel for twenty-three years. Then Jair, a Gileadite, was judge for twenty-two years. For fifty years, the land knew peace under these judges.

But once again, the children of Israel *"did evil"* in the sight of the Lord. They served Baalim and Ashteroth, and the gods of Syria, and the gods of Zidon, and the gods of Moab, and the gods of the children of Ammon, and the gods of the Philistines. They *"forsook the LORD, and served not him"* (Judg. 10:6).

The anger of the Lord was hot against Israel, and this time, the enemies that rose up against them were the Philistines and the children of Ammon.

Have you noticed that the enemies God allowed to come against the Israelites came from different directions and in different combinations?

In the days of Othniel, the king of Mesopotamia put the Israelites into bondage. In the days of Ehud, the Moabites, joining forces with other enemies, caused the Israelites to suffer. In the days of Deborah and Barak, the Canaanites oppressed the Israelites with their nine hundred chariots. In Gideon's time, the Midianites oppressed the people.

The Israelites didn't face the same enemy time after time—they faced different enemies coming from different directions.

Never think that just because you have been delivered from one enemy in your life, you are going to sail all the way to heaven on a flowery bed of ease.

There's never any time when we are safe to let down our guard and give up our diligent, persistent pursuit of holiness.

The late Bishop J. O. Patterson used to say, "The devil is as full of tricks as a hound-dog is full of fleas."

Keep your eyes open!

Never Accept a Condition of Misery

This time, God allowed the Ammonites to come against Israel, and for eighteen years, the Ammonites *"vexed and oppressed"* the children of Israel on the east side of the Jordan. The Ammonites also crossed over the Jordan and fought against the tribes of Judah, Benjamin, and Ephraim so that *"Israel was sore distressed"* (Judg. 10:8–9).

- Vexed

- Oppressed

- Sore distressed

Can you imagine a more miserable trio of conditions to be in? To be vexed means to have your enemy continually needling away at you, finding every way possible to get to you.

To be vexed means to be in a constant state of being annoyed or irritated. It is a person's inner state.

Oppression comes at the hand of an oppressor. It is an outer state for a person. To be oppressed means that you are under the rule of a tyrant who creates an environment of misery for you. Conditions are hard to bear and heavy to the point of causing you to bow under the weight. Hunger, fatigue, poverty, and pain are four words that are often closely associated with oppression.

Too much outward oppression, of course, can cause an inward oppression. It can result in deep mental anguish and a loss of hope. Many times the outward oppression of a human enemy can open the door to our experiencing spiritual oppression from the devil, who comes at us with such a weight of guilt and shame that we can hardly function.

Sore distressed is the outcome or the result of being vexed inwardly and oppressed outwardly. To be sore distressed means that you are in utter agony.

For eighteen years, the Israelites lived in a vexed, oppressed, sorely distressed state.

The amazing thing to me is that some people today don't really fight against conditions they find vexing. They put up with a tremendous amount of frustration, irritation, and annoyance from evil people.

Other people are all too quick to put up with conditions that are difficult and hard—not just the normal course of work, but genuinely exhausting, debilitating conditions.

This was never God's plan for His people.

Yes, God wants us to work—diligently, persistently, giving our best.

Yes, God wants us to be patient and kind with people.

But God never calls us to allow evil people to run over us, irritate us to the point of tears, disrupt our worship services, or put such a heavy load upon us that we crumble in our minds, bodies, or spirits.

It is within the power of your free will to cry for deliverance. Do so!

It is within the power of your free will to choose to trust God to bring you out from such bondage and misery. Do so!

Never lose sight of the fact that God has given you a free will and faith. Use them to bring forth your best effort and to believe for God's finest victory. And then, give all glory to God!

Never Lose Sight of the Power of Your Choice

Anytime you are confronted with misery, remember that it is within the power of your free will, given to you by your Creator, to choose to worship God and to choose to obey His commandments. It is within the power of your will to believe for freedom

Barrabas- son of humility

and deliverance. Your exercise of free will, and your believing with your faith, is often summed up in one word: choice.

God will not make your choices for you when it comes to whom you worship, what you believe for, and how you obey.

Pilate said to the crowds gathered to witness the trial of Jesus, *"Whom will ye that I release unto you? Barabbas, or Jesus which is called Christ?"* (Matt. 27:17).

The people chose Barabbas. The name *Barabbas* literally means "son of humanity"—he was the "son of the fathers."

The people chose the son of the fathers instead of the Son of Divinity, the Son of the Father, the Son of God.

Countless people today are choosing to follow humanity—men and women who are mere sons of humanity, possessions and positions that are the inventions of humanity, creations of the human mind, and emotions of the human heart.

God calls us to choose His divinity—to follow His only begotten Son, His eternal plan and purpose, His commandments and statutes that are for our good.

Have you made your choice?

Is your choice a firm commitment?

Are you living out your commitment in obedience?

Is your obedience producing a life of purity and holiness?

The choice is yours!

Five Things You Must Choose

There are five things you must choose to do in your life—not just once, but consistently from day to day, month to month, year to year. These are ongoing choices that God gives to you. They are choices you must make for your own life.

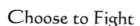

Choose to Fight

First, you must choose to fight. Yes, fight for yourself, fight for your family, fight for your integrity, fight for your health! Don't lie down and let the enemy walk all over your life. And on the flip side, don't expect God to divinely solve all your problems in an instant. Too many people are falling down in fear before the devil and standing up in pride before God when we need to be standing up in strength before the devil and falling on our faces in humility before God.

Now, God may heal your body instantly or turn things around in a situation so that it will seem that the change came instantly, but even sick people who are healed instantly need to regain their strength and learn how to walk in the vitality of their healing. Even marriages that start to be turned around in a conversation need to be rebuilt in areas of trust and responsibility and ongoing commitment. Even emotional breakthroughs need to be lived out, with readjustments and new behaviors that are built upon truth, instead of lies.

Face up to the fact that you have a part in regaining whatever it is that you are presently in the process of losing; you have a part in going from a status of losing to a status of winning.

Choose to Learn God's Plan

Second, you must know what it is that God wants you to have and how He wants you to live. To know that, you must choose to become informed.

You need to know His promises to you. He's given you those promises in His Word. The commandments and judgments of God are very clear. They are available for you to read in a number of versions and translations and bindings and typefaces, with notes and red letters and maps and illustrations and cross references. Before you can win the war that's being waged against you, you need to have a clear vision of what victory looks like.

You need to know on the basis of God's Word—not on the basis of some TV talk show guest or radio psychologist or neighbor or relative—exactly what it is that God desires for you. You need to have a clear vision of what the Promised Land looks like and what the boundaries of it are.

Knowing what God wants you to have makes it clear what God doesn't want you to have. God wants you to have energy and vitality and strength, which means He doesn't want you to have that debilitating headache that recurs every few days. God wants you to have a healthy and mutually enjoyable marriage, which means He doesn't want you to have that lover on the side. God wants you to walk in confidence, boldly entering His throne room, which means He doesn't want you paralyzed by fear.

God's Word is very clear. The Bible says "do this" and "don't do that." In order to claim all the promises of God, you've got to know what is promised to you and what isn't.

Choose to Face Your Spiritual Enemy

Third, you must recognize that the enemy that desires to keep you from possessing all of the promises of God is a spiritual enemy. You must choose to do spiritual battle against the enemy of your soul.

The person or group that is coming against you is not your real enemy. Your real enemy is unseen and far greater than the person or group that is standing in your way, putting you down, pushing you aside, pulling you under, or rolling over you. To win a spiritual battle, you need to deal in spiritual matters and use spiritual methods.

There's very little benefit in getting angry or bitter or frustrated at a person. Save all that for getting mad at the devil.

In fact, God's Word says we are to love our enemies and do good to those who persecute us. One reason for that is there's still a possibility our enemies might turn to Christ and cease to be our enemies. Another reason for that is that love takes a whole lot less time and emotional energy than revenge. Love is a lot better feeling than hate. Love builds up and is effective in bringing about healing and restoration—hate tears down and causes even wider gaps in a relationship. I choose love in Jesus name

Yes, love your enemies and hate the devil. At no time are we to compromise with the devil, bow to him, or be kind to him. We are to take him on in battle and win. We do that to a great extent by praising God and worshipping Him with our entire body, mind, and spirit.

There's very little to be gained by sitting down in despair and feeling frustrated, sad, or rejected that nobody is helping you. Get on your feet and start praising God from whom all blessings flow!

As you own up to your real enemy in the spiritual realm, also recognize that there's a spiritual root to every problem. For any problem to be completely solved, you have to deal with that spiritual root.

Gardeners know this. Cut off just the top of a weed and that weed will be back in a hurry. It's only when you pull the weed out by its root that you get rid of the weed. And the only way to regain the soil where that weed existed and to ensure that a weed doesn't grow there again is to put in a good plant to take up that soil. Which leads me to my next point....

Choose to Discover God's Plan for Your Delivered Life

Fourth, in order for you to live in God's blessings, you've got to learn how God intends for you to live after your deliverance. You have to choose a new pattern of purity, holiness, and obedience.

You've got to know what to plant in place of that addiction in your life. You've got to know what kinds of friendships and relationships to build into your life in place of the bad friendships and sick relationships that are enticing you to sin. You've got to know what to put into your life to take up those hours that you sit in loneliness. And most importantly, you must know what you need to put off and put on spiritually. The apostle Paul wrote to the Ephesians:

> *Put off...the old man, which is corrupt according to the deceitful lusts; and be renewed in the spirit of your mind; and that ye put on the new man, which after God is created in righteousness and true holiness.* (Eph. 4:22–24)

God does not foist His holiness on you, or place His righteousness on you like a mantle falling on your shoulders. The putting off and putting on are our responsibility. Do you know today what you need to put off in order to get rid of that enemy that is plaguing your life—the spirit of poverty, lust, greed, doubt, fear, anger, or self-exaltation? Do you know what you need to put on in order to live a life that does not grieve the Holy Spirit, but rather, brings glory to God? Do you know what to put on in order to walk before the Lord blameless, and thus be in position to receive all the blessings He wants to pour out on your life?

Choose to Discern God's Methods and Timing

Fifth and finally, you've got to discern God's methods and timing. You must choose to listen to the Lord until He tells you when to go and how to proceed.

Some things need to be done immediately. Some things need to be done first. Some things need to be done in conjunction with other things. Some things need to be done over time.

The Israelites didn't take on the whole land of Canaan in the same week. They took on the city nearest to the point where they crossed over the Jordan River. That city was Jericho, which is about fourteen miles east of Jerusalem. From there, they moved on to the city of Ai, which was about ten miles north of Jerusalem. Then they went to the south. And then they engaged in the northern campaign. The conquest was orderly. It was in God's ordained sequence. It was according to God's methods. And very

Don't Put Up With Misery

importantly, no tribe operated on its own. Even those tribes that were eventually going to settle on the east side of the Jordan River crossed over and helped all of the other tribes fight the battles that would claim Canaan for the Israelites as a whole.

Note Can you see the application in your life?

① God has a starting point for your battle and He has an ending place of victory. In between, He has a strategy that you need to discover as you pray and study God's Word and listen closely to the Holy Spirit speaking within your spirit. There's a precision to God's methods and His timing. It's up to you to do the discerning.

O In summary, this is your part:

- Be willing to fight.
- Know who you are ultimately fighting against.
- Know what you need to do to prepare for the battle.
- Know the goal you're fighting for.
- Know where, when, and how to fight.

If you will do these things—all in the context of listening to God, worshipping God, and obeying God—you will take the land. You will conquer the enemies that are arrayed against you.

And yet there's more....

It's not enough to conquer the land. You've got to claim the land and keep claiming it.

An Ongoing Claiming of the Promised Land

Key strongholds were defeated by the combined armies of the twelve tribes of Israel. Then, toward the end of Joshua's life, the tribes were sent to their assigned plots of land. They went knowing that they faced the challenge of occupying the land and continuing the conquest of minor enemies and hold-out strongholds. Not all of the Canaanite strongholds had been taken by Joshua and the twelve tribes. Certain ones, those less vital to the overall conquest but nonetheless real and strong, had been bypassed. The individual tribes were expected to fight against these pockets of enemy strength and occupy their territories.

As the tribes moved to the specific areas assigned to them by God through Moses, they found they still had more fighting to do to fully claim their allotted space. Their enemies didn't flee before them. There was no instant peace. A great many battles still had to be fought. God's promise was an ongoing promise of victory—but it was a guaranteed victory that still required the Israelites to have courage, to obey God's commands, and to fight.

Occupying the land meant just that—occupying. Physically and literally, the Israelites drove out their enemies and then occupied their empty dwellings, places of business, and farms. As part of the process they had to take on the housekeeping and the running of a permanent place of residence (not just a tent), the running of businesses (including some, such as masonry, that they hadn't needed to know in the wilderness), the hard work of working in vineyards and orchards (which they didn't have in the wilderness), and managing livestock on permanent pastures.

All of these things were a blessing to the Israelites. But they also meant work. And not only that, but these blessings also meant a major shift in thinking. At that point, the Israelites had been a nomadic people for almost two full generations—the generation that left Egypt (all of whom died in the wilderness except Joshua and Caleb), and the generation that entered the land and conquered it. In a matter of months, the Israelites needed to learn how to be a "settled down" people—settled in permanent dwellings, living in permanent cities, farming crops, and establishing long-term plans and goals. They had to develop new routines, new responsibilities, and in some cases, new careers.

The Lord knew there was a lot of work yet to be done before Canaan would be fully claimed.

Near the time of Joshua's death, the Lord said to Joshua, *"There remaineth yet very much land to be possessed"* (Josh. 13:1). The Lord identified the borders and territories still to be conquered and said to Joshua about the inhabitants of these areas, *"Them will I drive out from before the children of Israel: only divide thou it by lot unto the Israelites for an inheritance, as I have commanded thee"* (v. 6). Note this

The same thing is true for us who are followers of our Lord Jesus Christ. All of our problems were not removed the day we accepted Jesus as our Savior or received the Holy Spirit into our lives. All of our enemies, addictions, sicknesses, weaknesses, faults, failures, and flaws didn't evaporate into thin air. However, our sins were cleansed in a moment. Our spiritual nature was changed forever in an instant. We moved from death to life immediately, just as a baby comes out of the womb and suddenly is subject to gravity and has to breathe on its own.

Our spiritual nature and eternal destiny changed with our salvation and sanctification—but much of the rest of our lives was not changed. Our personalities and habits and associations weren't overthrown or replaced. The day after we accepted Christ, we still woke up in the same fallen world. Some of us found we were still living with the same fallen spouses in the same broken-down houses and dealing with the same failing projects.

The big enemy of our lives—the devil—had been defeated on the matter of our eternal souls. We went from being the slaves of the devil to being the treasured possession of God. But we weren't immunized from attacks by the devil and his demons. We weren't removed from the possibility of temptation or trial or trouble.

There was still land to claim. There were battles to fight and win. There were new ways of thinking and believing to be established, a process the Bible calls the renewal of our old minds, which had developed a tendency to consistently think wrong, negative, or sinful thoughts. There were new routines we had to build into our lives and new connections we had to make, sometimes with a new set of people. There were new schedules we had to make to include worship and ministry, new habits we had to adopt, and new ways of responding we had to develop and employ.

Furthermore, the land we claimed after we were saved and sanctified is land that we must still claim. No person ever gets beyond being tempted. (It's not a sin to be tempted—it's a sin to give in to temptation. There's nothing you can ever do to fully immunize yourself from being tempted.)

No person ever gets beyond the possibility of making a wrong decision or hurting someone else without meaning to.

No person ever gets beyond the capacity for making a mistake.

The potential is always there to slip and fall and do what we genuinely don't want to do.

- Purity must be the choice we make. I choose purity
- Holiness must be the choice we make. holiness is my choise
- Righteousness must be the choice we make. I is Righteous
- Obedience must be the choice we make. I obey
- Trust in God must be the choice we make. trust

Not just once—but today and always. EVERy day
I Choose
Life
my Papa God
my Jesus.
& the my holy spirit
Tues. March 12-24
5:20 am.

13

God Loves You Enough to Change You and Use You

One of the greatest truths of the Gospel of Jesus Christ is that God accepts every sinner who repents. He accepts us just as we are.

An equally great truth is that God doesn't leave us where we are. He causes us to be "born again" in our spirits. He conforms us into the character likeness of Christ Jesus. He renews our minds. He changes us and makes us "new creatures." (See John 3:3–6; Romans 8:29; 12:2; 2 Corinthians 5:17.)

God not only transforms us, but He also uses us at every point in our transformation. He doesn't wait until we get "good enough" for ministry. He calls upon us to be a witness to His saving grace from the first hour of our salvation. He uses us in the gifts of the Spirit from the hour we receive the Spirit.

God loves us enough to change us and use us.

That's one of the great lessons we can learn from the life of a judge over the Israelites—a man named Jephthah.

Jephthah was a Gileadite, and, like Gideon, he is described in the Bible as a mighty man of valor.

Jephthah was also the son of a harlot. Nobody questioned that Jephthah was the son of Gilead. Everybody knew that, including Gilead's wife and his half brothers. When his half brothers grew up, however, they cast Jephthah from the family and said, *"Thou shalt not inherit in our father's house; for thou art the son of a strange woman"* (Judg. 11:2).

Jephthah fled from the area and dwelt in the land of Tob. Gilead was part of the area given to the tribe of Manasseh. This part of the Promised Land was on the east side of the Jordan River, along the Jordan River, north of the territory occupied by the Ammonites. Today it is a very lush part of the nation of Jordan.

When Jephthah left, he went north about twenty miles, and there a group of men saw that he had leadership qualities, and they made him their leader. The men who aligned themselves with Jephthah were not unlike gang members today who tend to rally around a person who shows some leadership ability. These men who associated with Jephthah are described in the Bible as "worthless" men, most of whom had also been cast out of their families for a variety of reasons.

Then the day came when the Ammonites made war against Israel, and they moved directly north toward Gilead.

The Gileadites looked around at all of the so-called legitimate children in the area and didn't see any one who could lead them in the fight against the Ammonites. Finally, the elders of Gilead sent for Jephthah.

Be Careful Who You Cast Out

Be careful who you cast out of your life, your family, your church, or your community. Be careful who you label as being unworthy of association with you. Be careful who you dismiss as being unredeemable, unlovable, unacceptable, and undeserving. Down the line, you may find that God calls you to open your arms to that person.

The truth is that no person is unlovable in God's eyes. God extends His unconditional love and mercy to all people, including those whom we tend to find the most despicable. The Bible tells us plainly that *"God commendeth his love toward us, in that, while we were yet sinners, Christ died for us"* (Rom. 5:8). No person is unlovable in God's eyes, and neither should any person be perceived as unlovable or unredeemable in our eyes. The Bible also says to us, *"If God so loved us, we ought also to love one another"* (1 John 4:11).

When it comes to being worthy of God's love, none of us was worthy initially. We all were sinners deserving death. It is Christ Jesus who has made us worthy—our worthiness is nothing we can generate or claim in ourselves. God says we are worthy of the death of His Son, and when we receive Jesus into our lives as our Savior, God says we are worthy of eternal life. When we trust Jesus as our Lord, God says we are worthy to become joint heirs with Christ. No person who is your brother or sister in Christ is unworthy of your association, assistance, or fellowship.

Jephthah was a son of Gilead and had a right to be treated as a son of Gilead, regardless of who his mother may have been. There are many people today who are judged and cast out of the presence of God's people because they don't fit the standard that a certain group of people have set up for themselves. We need always to ask ourselves in our treatment of other people, "Is this God's standard of good behavior? Or is this my own prejudice rising up and showing its ugly self? Is this my own self-seeking nature at work?"

The brothers of Jephthah didn't like what was in Jephthah's background. Let me assure you of this—everyone has something in his or her background that someone isn't going to like or approve. Jesus had something in His background that the Pharisees didn't like—and it had to do with His birth.

The Pharisees said to Jesus, *"Abraham is our father."* Jesus replied, *"If ye were Abraham's children, ye would do the works of Abraham. But now ye seek to kill me, a man that hath told you the truth, which I have heard of God: this did not Abraham. Ye do the deeds of your father."* Then they said back to Jesus, *"We be not born of fornication; we have one Father, even God."* And Jesus said, *"If God were your Father, ye would love me: for I proceeded forth and came from God; neither came I of myself, but he sent me"* (John 8:39–42).

The Pharisees questioned Jesus' legitimacy—both in the physical and in the spiritual realm.

Let me remind you of some things that you can count on as being true for every person on this earth: God created that person; God allowed that person to be born, and He did so with an expressed purpose in mind. God wants to redeem every person He creates.

Let me also remind you that every person who has accepted Jesus Christ as Savior is your brother or sister in Christ. We don't get to pick and choose the people God saves and redeems by His shed blood. We don't get a vote in selecting the people God sanctifies with His Holy Spirit. We don't get to help make the decision about the people God anoints with Holy Spirit power.

We in the church need to spend our energy and time trying to figure out how to get along with our fellow brothers and sisters in Christ Jesus, rather than spend that energy and time trying to figure out how to cast out some people so we will be "better off."

Note → If God has a design and purpose for your life, it doesn't matter how many human strikes you have against you.

It doesn't matter if your family rejects you.

It doesn't matter if the people at work don't like you.

It doesn't matter if the community casts you out.

If you love and serve God with all your heart, mind, and soul, God will take care of you. And He will bring you into the fullness and freedom He has created for you.

See Your Hardships as Preparation Times

The day came when the elders of Gilead called to Jephthah and said, *"Come, and be our captain, that we may fight with the children of Ammon"* (Judg. 11:6).

Take a new look at some of the hard times that come into your life. God may be using that very hardship to prepare you to take a leadership position later.

Romans 8:28 tells us, *"We know that all things work together for good to them that love God, to them who are the called according to his purpose."* This is a verse for Christians, not sinners. It is a verse for those who have accepted Jesus as their Savior. The good news is that, for Christians, all things are being worked together by God for good.

All means everything is included and nothing is excluded.

Even the painful situations, the negative circumstances, the suffering moments, the desert experiences, and the times of lack and loss are going to be used by God to strengthen you and bring you to a time and place that God calls good. Don't ever lose sight of that.

God doesn't say all things *are* good. He says all things are *working out* for your good. The laughter and the tears. The rainy days and the sunny days. The days with and the days without. The whole process ends in your favor.

A man once said, "I wouldn't take a million dollars for some experiences in my life. But you couldn't pay me a nickel to go back through those experiences." I couldn't agree more! Even so,

I know that all things have been, are now, and will be worked for my good because Jesus is my Savior and Lord. *Yes my Papa God*

What people see as a waste of time or the worst of times is actually what God often sees as preparation time. It's preparation time for something good. *help me Jesus to see You*

in what I'm going through HELP

Reason with Enemies? It Doesn't Work!

Jephthah said to the elders of Gilead, *"If ye bring me home again to fight against the children of Ammon, and the LORD deliver them before me, shall I be your head?"* (Judg. 11:9). And the elders of Gilead agreed.

Jephthah then tried to reason with the kings of the Ammonites. He challenged their false accusations with historical fact. And the Ammonites refused to acknowledge the truth.

Has that ever happened to you? Have you ever known the facts were on your side and tried to reason with an enemy? The fact is, enemies are our enemies because they want to destroy us, not live in peace with us. There's no reasoning with a genuine enemy. There's no way you can think your way into a peaceful coexistence with an enemy.

People who suffer from addictions and who have serious problems with doubt and fear often try to reason their way into dealing with these enemies of their lives.

They try to give justification for their fears and doubts. I recently heard about a woman who has a major fear—she refuses to get on an escalator or an elevator. She is scared to death of them; she goes into a cold sweat and gets the shakes if she has to even approach one. That's not of God. That's a binding fear. But when this woman was asked if she wanted God to deliver her from that fear, she said, "Oh, it's just a phobia." She didn't want to call it the spirit of fear or a binding fear or a paralyzing fear. She had chosen the word *phobia* to make her fear seem more justifiable and less serious.

If the devil can have such a strong hold on this woman's perceptions regarding escalators and elevators, what other strongholds is he likely to concoct regarding her perceptions about other things, more important things, even eternally important things?

This woman was trying to deal with an unreasonable fear in a reasonable way. It doesn't work.

I also heard not long ago about a man who has been addicted to nasal medications for several years. He has had to take more and more of the medications with less and less result, to the point where he can hardly get up in the morning without using a nasal spray first. When he was asked if he wanted to go to a service where people of faith would pray for his healing, he said, "Oh, that's not necessary. This is just my cross to bear. It's part of the disease I have."

This man thought his actions were reasonable, but they were an unreasonable approach to a terrible situation. It doesn't work!

When an enemy attacks, you can try reason if you want—but let me assure you, reason isn't going to work. You need the delivering power of God, not a treaty with your problem.

There's a teaching that's going around in our world today that we need to make peace with our own faults and failures. We need to accept our weaknesses, sins, and flaws as "just part of who we are." Those who advocate this say that we need to accept the way we are made and embrace ourselves as flawed human beings.

That's one hundred percent opposite of what Jesus taught. He said, *"Be ye therefore perfect, even as your Father which is in heaven is perfect"* (Matt. 5:48). The writer of Hebrews prayed, *"Now the God of peace...make you perfect in every good work to do his will, working in you that which is wellpleasing in his sight, through Jesus Christ"* (Heb. 13:20–21). By *"perfect,"* the Bible means whole or complete—whole in body, mind, spirit, and every other way. We aren't to accept sin, faults, weaknesses, or flaws as something we just have to put up with or, worse yet, come to like. We are to ask God to heal us, deliver us, change us, transform us, educate us, reconcile us, and perfect us. *Yes Jesus all of the*

Not

God intends for you, as a Christian, to always be in the process of being cleansed and changed and made into the very image of Jesus Christ, who had no sins or faults or weaknesses. (See Romans 8:29.)

God has something good in your future. *I except now*

God has perfection—completeness, wholeness—as His ultimate design for you. *thank you Papa God*

Don't try to reason your way into a compromise with anything less than God's total deliverance from your enemies. *ok*

Everyone May Not Rejoice in Your Deliverance

The king of the Ammonites did not listen to Jephthah but continued the assault. The Bible tells us, *"Then the Spirit of the LORD came upon Jephthah, and he passed over Gilead, and Manasseh, and passed over Mizpeh of Gilead, and from Mizpeh of Gilead he passed over"* (Judg. 11:29; see also verse 32).

Now you would think that would be the end of it. Jephthah had defeated the enemy and returned home the triumphant victor.

However, the Ephraimites were not happy about this.

The Ephraimites? They were a tribe of Israel. Even so, they were upset that Jephthah had gone to war against the Ammonites without consulting them first or inviting their participation. Jephthah responded that he had invited them, but they refused to come. (See Judges 12:1–4.) Most of us would say, "Hey, I'm glad they defeated the enemy without us. We didn't have to fight!"

That wasn't their response. They believed Jephthah had taken authority in the land of Israel that he should not have taken—not because he was an illegitimate son of Gilead, but because he was a Gileadite. They had a problem with his background, his people. Furthermore, they brought the Manassites into the picture, claiming that the Manassites were just as upset as the Ephraimites.

The fact was, Gilead was the grandson of Manasseh. (See Numbers 26:28–29.) The Gileadites were very much a legitimate part of the tribe of Manasseh, regardless of what the Ephraimites or the Manassites may have said.

Jephthah again tried to reason. He said, "I called you but you didn't respond. So I went ahead and fought." (See Judges 12:2–3.)

Again, reason and facts meant nothing. The elders of Ephraim wanted to be the ones to make any decision regarding war against the Ammonites. Perhaps some of them believed that if Jephthah had failed, they would have received the full force of the Ammonites' fury and been slaughtered in great numbers. Some of them, perhaps, just wanted to be in the power loop, the decision-making inner circle. Or maybe some of them were upset that they weren't going to get any of the glory that resulted from a defeat of the Ammonites.

The Bible doesn't tell us the exact reason the Ephraimites were so upset at Jephthah's victory, but we know all of those reasons exist in the human heart, not only then, but now.

In your life, if you defeat an enemy of your soul—whether it is fear, doubt, an addiction, victory over a particular sin, or whatever the enemy may be—there are likely to be some people who aren't happy about your deliverance. Some of them may even be members of your own family.

Certainly, if you have been a drug user or a drug dealer, your drug supplier or drug boss isn't going to be happy about your deliverance.

If you've been an alcoholic, the alcohol-related businesses aren't going to be excited about losing you as a customer.

If you are delivered from the sinful desires that have led to your involvement in a gang or mob, there will be people who are still in that gang or mob who aren't going to like your defection or your deliverance.

If you've been living in fear and haven't sought to develop your talents into usable skills, there are going to be people who don't like your deliverance. Some of them won't like the change in you because they don't like change, period. Some of them don't want you to be different—they had more control over you when you were uneducated. They were more able to manipulate you before you were freed from fear.

If you have been living in sin and you are delivered from sin and start going to church, there are going to be people who don't want you to leave their group and join up with a group of sanctified saints who aren't like them.

Your deliverance will upset somebody. Be prepared for that.

You May Need to Take Preemptive Measures

Most of those who oppose your deliverance aren't likely to be as upset as the Ephraimites, but some may be. The Ephraimites were so angry with Jephthah that they said they were on their way to burn his house down while he was still in it. (See Judges 12:1.)

Jephthah didn't wait for that to happen. He took a preventive measure—he embarked on a preemptive strike! He called the men of Gilead together and fought against Ephraim. The battle strategy called for him to take control of the crossing of the Jordan River. If any Ephraimite attempted to cross, the Gileadites had a way of identifying that man as an Ephraimite. They asked him to say the word *"Shibboleth."*

Now apparently there was something in the cultural use of the language in Ephraim that caused the Ephraimites to pronounce this word as "sibboleth" instead of "shibboleth." Some have speculated that the Ephraimites had an inability to hear the word correctly or to make the "sh" sound. Certainly we know that, even here in America, ethnic groups and people from different geographic locations have slightly different variations on the pronunciation of certain words. Whatever the cause, that one little speech difference was proof of Ephraimite identity.

Every Ephraimite who tried to cross over into Gilead was killed. And, in the end, forty-two thousand Ephraimites were slaughtered there by the Jordan. This no doubt was many times the number who actually fell in the battle against the Ammonites.

I pray you never have to take such drastic measures against an enemy who comes at you to kill and destroy you or your family. Let me point out this to you, however: Jephthah didn't wait for his enemies to attack him in this instance; he took measures to keep an attack from happening.

You may need to take measures to keep from being attacked by a secondary enemy after your deliverance from your primary enemy.

You may need to take a stand with your family, friends, or business associates and say, "Here's what happened. This is what God has done in my life. I don't want to argue about it or debate it. I'm choosing to follow Jesus Christ one hundred percent, and if you can't accept that, so be it. I'm committed to Christ now and forever."

You may need to disassociate yourself completely from those who had participated in your sin or who had been consenting to your bondage.

You will probably have to find things to do to fill the time you once gave to a bad habit or a sinful behavior. You might have to make new friends. You may need to find a new place of employment. You may need to drop some club memberships or give up frequenting some of the places where you used to go to relax. *OK Jesus guide me please*

Don't wait for those who don't like your deliverance to come up against you. Cut them off at the pass by your choices to pursue God's will for your life.

You won't have cash to buy something that had you in its addictive power if you have your money deposited directly into the bank and your bills paid directly from that account. You won't spend on the devil what you have already put into the offering plate at church. You won't have time to go with friends to the local bar or the place where your former friends hang out if you've already made an appointment with God to be at church or involved in a ministry. You won't be available to participate in an activity or association that had you in bondage if you've already left the house to spend time in a family activity.

You are going to have to make some changes in your life once you are delivered.

You may have to make some changes that you think of as being sacrifices—the changes may cost you something in terms of your former reputation, former spending habits, former participation, or former memberships.

There's one sacrifice, however, that you do not have to make, and that is the sacrifice of life—either your life or the life of someone you love.

Jephthah made that mistake as a judge. It's one you should never make.

Carefully Consider Every Vow You Make

Jephthah made a foolish vow, saying,

If thou shalt without fail deliver the children of Ammon into mine hands, then it shall be, that whatsoever cometh forth

*of the doors of my house to meet me, when I return in peace
from the children of Ammon, shall surely be the LORD's, and I
will offer it up for a burnt offering.* (Judg. 11:30–31)

God doesn't ask that we make any type of vow associated
with our deliverance. To make such a vow is like trying to bargain
with God, saying, "You do this, and I'll do that." Or, "I'll do this, and
then You will be obligated to do that."

God doesn't bargain. God is the One who sets the rules and
boundaries, develops the plan, and bestows His Spirit. He is the
Captain of our souls. We are in a position of obeying or disobeying,
but never bargaining. *Yes I want to obey papa*

It was enough that the Spirit of the Lord had come upon
Jephthah. That's all he needed to know in order to obey. God neither required a vow from him, or responded to the vow Jephthah
made. The Spirit of the Lord wasn't contingent on a vow; it wasn't
given to Jephthah on the basis of a vow.

Once a vow is made to the Lord, however, it must be kept.
help me to follow
That's the Law of Moses. Vows are voluntary, but they are determined to be very important. There are a number of admonitions
in the Old Testament about a person "paying the vows" he or she
makes to the Lord. (See Deuteronomy 23:23 and Ecclessiastes 5:4
as examples.) In fact, in Ecclesiastes we find this caution against
making hasty vows: *"Better is it that thou shouldest not vow, than
that thou shouldest vow and not pay. Suffer not thy mouth to cause
thy flesh to sin"* (Eccl. 5:5–6). *help me to obey; follow you my Jesus; hold me keep me*

When Jephthah returned home, he was horrified to find that
the first one to greet him was his beloved daughter, who came out *need*
to meet him with timbrels and dancing. He had vowed to sacrifice *you*
"whatsoever" came first from the doors of his house to meet him.
He hadn't counted on *"whatsoever"* being "whomsoever" in the
form of his only daughter. The moment he saw her, he tore his
clothes as a sign of deep regret and mourning and cried, *"Alas! I*
I don't want to make no foolish vow NO

have opened my mouth unto the Lord, and I cannot go back on my vow." (See Judges 11:34–35.)

There are some who believe this girl just remained single the rest of her life, and there are others who believe Jephthah actually sacrificed her to the Lord, but in either case, the result was that Jephthah's line of blood descendants was cut off. He had no other heirs. The line of Jephthah died out in the aftermath of that vow. *Pray Papa God help me follow your will*

Never make a vow in your ignorance that is totally outside God's will. There was only one human sacrifice required by God, and that was the sacrifice of Jesus Christ on the cross, dying for our sins. God called upon Abraham to offer his son, but God knew when He tested Abraham that He was not going to take Isaac. An angel called to Abraham out of heaven and caused him to stay his hand and take the ram in the thicket as the sacrifice in Isaac's place. That was a symbol of Jesus' becoming our substitute sacrifice. God never required human sacrifice from His people. He doesn't require it now.

When you are delivered from your enemy, don't run from your spouse or your children. God hasn't delivered you from them. He has delivered you so you might be restored to them, love them, and build a renewed relationship with them. Ask God to show you how to heal your broken relationship with your spouse or your children. No person suffers from an enemy on his own—the entire family is always involved. When deliverance comes, it's a deliverance God intends for the entire family. *Amen Jesus*

If you abandon your children or your spouse in the wake of your deliverance, you are killing your relationship with them, and, in the process, you are killing something inside them that God never intended to be killed. You will be killing their capacity to trust, to love, to make and keep a commitment, to learn how to reconcile. Your leaving will always cause far more harm than good. Your staying and trusting God to heal the entire family and deliver the family from evil is the only way genuine healing and wholeness can occur.

A Public Victory, A Private Loss

Jephthah was a man who did not allow God to change him. He was used by God to bring a great deliverance to the Israelites. His victory was public and widespread. He judged Israel for six years.

His private life, however, was a tragedy. He ran with the wrong crowd. He made a vow that cost him his future heirs.

There are countless people today whom God uses mightily to bring deliverance to His people. Their public life and ministry is a great success. At home, however, things aren't right. God uses these men and women to change others, but the sad tragedy is that they never allow God to change them and make them into the fathers, husbands, mothers, or friends that God desires for them to be. *Change me Papa God change me - 3-14-24 7:18pm Thursday Don't let me go I need you.*

We must never assume that because God is using us, He has ceased to desire to change us. Until the day we can stand as a perfect mirror image of the character of Christ Jesus—a day that will come in eternity—we must always bend our knee to the Lord and pray, "Not my will, but Yours. Not my choices, but Yours. Not my fleshly nature, but Your nature. Not by my spirit, but by Your Spirit." *Thank you Papa God for give me Your will*

Trust God today to transform you so He can better use you. *to make my choice to serve you Love you trust you obey you help me Papa God in you Son Jesus name I need deliver I claim my deliverance tonight Now in Jesus name Holy Spirit Comfort me I need you* 183 *3-14-24 7:21pm Hallelujah*

14

Avoiding the Need to Fight

After six years of judging the Israelites, Jephthah the Gileadite died and was buried in one of the cities of Gilead. He was followed by Ibzan, Elon, and Abdon—three judges who spanned twenty-five years.

No mention is made of any enemies that sought to invade the Promised Land during this time of judges Ibzan, Elon, and Abdon—there is no mention of any enemies who were defeated. These judges apparently were strong men who gave sound leadership and taught their children to love and serve the Lord.

In the case of Ibzan, that was no easy feat. Ibzan had thirty sons and thirty daughters, and he arranged marriages for all of them. (See Judges 12:9.)

The Best Testimony

One of the greatest testimonies that any person can have is that he does not fall into sin or worship a false god, but rather that he loves and serves God every day of his life.

So often we tend to think that having a testimony means that we have fallen into deep sin and then been saved or delivered by God. That's one testimony, and it is always good when a person is saved

Note

or delivered from sin. But the best testimony is to love and serve God with a pure heart and never fall into sin or backslide in the first place.

God cares deeply about your holiness. *Holiness* means, "separated, consecrated, dedicated, and set apart for God's purposes." It also means to be pure, or untainted by evil or sin.

God wants His people to live in holiness. He wants us to seek Him with our whole being—mind, spirit, soul, and body. He wants us to worship Him as our first priority. He wants us to be so intent on doing His will and walking in His ways that we won't even entertain the thought of checking out a false god or dabbling in a false religion. *Don't entertain thoughts BIND them NOW*

Note Did God take pleasure in seeing His people suffer under their enemies? Did God take pleasure in seeing His people have to go to war against their enemies? Never! God wanted His people to enter the land that He had promised to them, trust Him to drive out their enemies from before them, trust Him to help them occupy the land and develop it and flourish in it, and trust Him to show them what they needed to do to secure their lives, and their borders, from any enemy attack. God's plan was never that they should worship false gods, fall into bondage, and then need to be delivered. He wanted them to trust Him so He might bless them and build them up and keep them from all harm. *Hallelujah! Jesus*

Sometimes we get so caught up in trying to avoid sin—or we get so caught up in trying to figure out how to disentangle ourselves from a problem—that we fail to see the big picture of what we should be doing. *Now help me Jesus*

Regaining a Picture of What We Should Do

What is it we should be doing?

Let me remind you of some of the basics.

God calls His people to go to church—not just occasionally, but regularly. As far as I am concerned, you ought to be in the

Yes

best church in your city. Get yourself surrounded by the most Holy Spirit-filled, worshipping people you can find. Get involved with those people and get involved in their outreach ministries to the lost, sick, imprisoned, and poor. Find a place within that church to serve. Find a place within that church where you can be taught the deeper truths of the Word of God. And then stick there. Don't wander away from it.

God calls His people to know His Word. To know His Word, you've got to read and study your Bible faithfully and diligently. You've got to weigh everything you hear against what you read in the Bible. The Bible is God's truth—choose to read the truth, heed the truth, and spread the truth. Yes

God calls His people to talk to Him—again and again throughout any given day. Give God your thanksgiving and praise from morning to night. Pray to the Lord, asking Him for the things you need. Intercede in prayer on behalf of others. Ask the Holy Spirit to help you make decisions, solve problems, and give you guidance as to where you should go, what you should do, how, and when.

God calls His people to love one another. He tells us to give to those in need, to walk in fellowship with one another, to be generous in hospitality, and to have an attitude of mercy and patience toward all who are in the body of Christ.

God calls His people to tell the lost about Jesus Christ. He invites us to be His witnesses, His ambassadors, His emissaries to a lost and dying world.

God calls His people to work quietly and diligently at the tasks He puts before them. He calls His people to obey the authorities in the land, even as they pray for those authorities. He calls His people to serve Him with their gifts—their tithes and offerings and their giving of talents and service—so His work might go forward.

If we are busy and fully occupied in doing what we should be doing, we will have neither the time nor the energy to get involved in things we should not be doing. Neither will we have the inclination to pursue those things. *help me Papa God*

If you are going to church on Sunday and once during the week, reading your Bible daily, spending time talking to the Lord and listening to the Lord each day, doing the work God calls you to do, involved in a ministry God calls you to be involved in, loving your family and friends and neighbors and fellow saints in the church as best you know how, telling the lost about Jesus, living in obedience and trusting God in every area of your life, giving your tithes and offerings faithfully, and seeking to be conformed in all ways to the image of Christ Jesus, you will be fully engaged in all that is required for God to unfold His blessings upon you and to give you the fullness of the inheritance He has authorized for you in your promised land. He will defeat your enemies, without you even knowing that an attack has been launched against you. He will protect you, provide for you, and guard you on all fronts. *thank you Jesus*

Does that mean that you will never experience any sadness, sorrow, sickness, or loss? No. We live in a fallen world, and we must always remember that the Promised Land was still on this earth. Weeds still grew in the Promised Land, earthquakes still shook the earth, floods still caused rivers and creek beds to overflow, and wild animals still killed innocent sheep. God said to His people, however, that those who served Him fully would find that He rebuked the devourer for their sakes so that they would not be destroyed. (See Malachi 3:11.) At the same time, the Lord promised to send such an abundance that His people would have more than they could use, which would allow them to help others all around them with a genuine generosity of heart.

God's Promise of Abundant Life

Hard patches may come, but the overall trend in the life of every person who pursues the holiness of God is going to be a

Note

trend in which devourers are rebuked and blessings are bestowed. The life Jesus calls us to is an abundant life. (See John 10:10.) It is a life marked by holiness and wholeness.

Praise God today if your life isn't being attacked by an enemy. Praise God for the state of deliverance in which you find yourself. And stay faithful to Him. Don't let your love for Him grow cold. Don't let your hands get weary in their well-doing.

- Continue to work and build in the promised land He has given you!

- Continue to keep His commandments!

- Continue to worship Him with your whole heart!

- Continue to anticipate with delight the good things He is preparing for you and the perfection He is creating inside you!

Keep Your Eyes on the Lord

Keep your eyes on God's holiness and perfection! Never take your focus off of all that God is, all that God created you to be, and all that God calls you to be in Christ Jesus. Never lose hope in all that God is preparing for you. Never lose sight of all that God desires to be and to do on your behalf.

Isaiah had such a vision. He saw the Lord sitting on His throne and all His holy angels surrounding Him with cries of *"Holy, holy, holy, is the LORD of hosts: the whole earth is full of his glory"* (Isa. 6:3).

Isaiah responded, *"Woe is me! for I am undone; because I am a man of unclean lips, and I dwell in the midst of a people of unclean lips: for mine eyes have seen the King, the LORD of hosts"* (Isa. 6:5).

Isaiah recognized that he wasn't saying what the angels in heaven were saying. He recognized his sin and his shortcomings.

He saw his environment and his associations for what they were. He felt *"undone"!*

And in that state of humble confession and repentance, Isaiah experienced the purging of his sin at God's sovereign hand. He saw an angel carrying a live coal from the altar of heaven and placing that coal upon his mouth. He heard the angel say to him, *"Lo, this hath touched thy lips; and thine iniquity is taken away, and thy sin purged"* (Isa. 6:7). Isaiah knew what it meant to be forgiven by God. He knew he had been cleansed of all that he had said and done that was displeasing to God.

Then Isaiah heard the Lord say, *"Whom shall I send, and who will go for us?"* And Isaiah responded, *"Here am I; send me"* (v. 8). It wasn't enough that he was forgiven. There was something Isaiah was to do. Forgiveness is a state; ministry is action.

God calls all those whom He saves to be His witnesses—to spread the Gospel, preach to those who haven't heard about Jesus, to heal the sick, to cleanse the lepers (and restore all who are outcast), raise the dead (and those who are the walking dead, the dead in despair without hope), and to cast out demons. (See Matthew 10:7–8.)

Isaiah was willing to go. God said, *"Go"* (Isa. 6:9). He didn't promise the people would understand him or heed what he had to say. And God doesn't promise us results either. The results are His business. Our part is the going and telling.

Throughout your life you are going to come to moments and situations in which you suddenly catch a glimpse of God's perfect plan and you are going to be caught short. You are going to feel a pain in your conscience—you are going to find yourself saying, "I should have," "I could have," "I ought to have," "I might have."

When those moments come, quickly go to God and confess, "Woe is me! I have allowed myself to speak with unclean lips and to get myself into the midst of a people who aren't living for You.

Help me! I see the error of my ways. Rescue me from this situation and from my own sinful impulses and desires."

God will hear you and answer you. He will forgive you. But then He will ask you, "Are you willing now to be My person on this earth? Are you willing to live in holiness before Me? Are you willing to keep My commandments and worship Me with your whole heart?"

God wants your answer to be "Yes! Send me to be Your person. Make me to be Your man or Your woman on this earth, in my home, in my church, and in my community."

Keep your eyes on the Lord and go in the name of the Lord. Live for Him, regardless of how others around you live. Speak for Him words of mercy and forgiveness, joy and peace; love others for His sake; give to others in His name.

Keep your focus on His glory and His holiness.

A Pattern of Repentance, Purity, and Praise

The big picture of God's pattern for us is this: repentance, cleansing, walking in obedience and purity, and praise. God calls us to move from sin to holiness, and as we are transformed and renewed by His Spirit, we are to live in great joy.

Again and again throughout the book of Judges, we find that God's people cried to Him out of their need, confessing their sin to Him and asking Him to forgive. And again and again, we find that God forgives and cleanses the repentant, and then calls His people to activate their faith, pursue purity and holiness in their obedience, and give Him thanksgiving and praise. It's not only a pattern in the book of Judges, but it's a pattern that's in the Bible story after story, book after book.

Repentance

In the book of Judges, one of the recurring refrains is this: *"And when the children of Israel cried unto the LORD, the LORD raised up a deliverer to the children of Israel"* (Judg. 3:9).

The children of Israel cried! Their cries were ones of desperation, deep sorrow, and despair—they cried from the very depths of their souls.

Note that they didn't just cry. A lot of us today are in trouble and we cry, but that's all we do. We cry. We curl up in our pillows and we cry. That kind of crying may give a little, temporary emotional relief, but it doesn't bring lasting deliverance.

Some of us who are in trouble start crying to other folk. We find a shoulder to lean on and we cry. Some people cry to just about anyone who will listen. Some people even cry to total strangers on national television talk shows. That kind of crying may result in a little temporary help from someone, a little solace or a little sympathy, but it doesn't bring lasting deliverance. The children of Israel didn't just cry—they cried to the Lord. *Help me Lord*

For all of their faults, we at least must credit the Israelites with this: When they got into deep trouble beyond their ability to endure it any longer, they had the good sense to cry out to the Lord. *Amen*

They didn't cry out to their enemies or against their enemies. They didn't cry out to the government or to the local welfare agency. They didn't cry out to the news media. They cried to the Lord.

They cried out to the only One who could genuinely, sovereignly, supernaturally, definitively help them. *Hallelujah me too*

That's true for you and me today. Agencies and organizations are fine, and they have their role in our society, but the only lasting deliverance from the troubles that truly plague us from the inside out is the deliverance we get from God Almighty.

Cry out to God.

And very specifically, cry out in repentance.

- Cry out with a heart that truly desires to experience the mercy and forgiveness of God!

- Cry out with a heart that is remorseful for sin and error!

- Cry out with a heart that longs for the presence of God!

- Cry out with a heart that seeks a total deliverance from all the devil's principalities and power!

The Bible says repeatedly that when the Israelites cried out to God, He raised up a judge to deliver the people.

God's response to a truly repentant heart is always a move toward forgiveness, deliverance, and a rebuilding of human life in the likeness of Christ Jesus.

Every time you come before the Lord on a matter, come with a humble, repentant heart. Ask God to cleanse you and forgive you completely from sin in your life. Acknowledge everything you know that is contrary to God's commandments, and then ask God to reveal to you what you haven't recognized as a sin or what you may be forgetting (consciously or unconsciously) is a sin. And as God reveals other sins to you, confess them, repent of them, and be forgiven for them.

As a man once said, "Every sin you confess on this earth is one less sin that is counted against your life when you get to heaven." Ask God to reveal all that you need to confess to Him and turn away from.

Cleansing

Our confession of sin results in God's cleansing of our sin. John wrote, *"If we confess our sins, he is faithful and just to forgive us our sins, and to cleanse us from all unrighteousness"* (1 John 1:9).

God's desire is always to cleanse you from sin.

After David had sinned with Bath-sheba and sent Uriah, Bath-sheba's husband, to death on the front lines of battle, he was confronted by the prophet Nathan. Rather than try to justify his sin, David cried out to the Lord:

> Have mercy upon me, O God, according to thy lovingkindness: according unto the multitude of thy tender mercies blot out my transgressions. Wash me thoroughly from mine iniquity, and cleanse me from my sin....Purge me with hyssop, and I shall be clean: wash me, and I shall be whiter than snow....Create in me a clean heart, O God; and renew a right spirit within me. Cast me not away from thy presence; and take not thy holy spirit from me. Restore unto me the joy of thy salvation; and uphold me with thy free spirit. (Ps. 51:1–2, 7, 10–12)

Throughout the Bible, God promises to cleanse those who come to him with a heart that is repentant:

• *Come now, and let us reason together, saith the* LORD: *though your sins be as scarlet, they shall be as white as snow; though they be red like crimson, they shall be as wool. If ye be willing and obedient, ye shall eat the good of the land.* (Isa. 1:18–19)

• [Thus saith the LORD]: *I will cleanse them from all their iniquity, whereby they have sinned against me; and I will pardon all their iniquities, whereby they have sinned, and whereby they have transgressed against me.* (Jer. 33:8)

• [Thus saith the Lord GOD]: *For I will take you from among the heathen, and gather you out of all countries, and will bring you into your own land. Then will I sprinkle clean water upon you, and ye shall be clean: from all your filthiness, and from all your idols, will I cleanse you. A new heart also will I give you, and a new spirit will I put within you: and I will take away the stony heart out of your flesh, and I will give you an heart of flesh. And I will put my spirit within you, and cause you to walk in my statutes, and ye shall keep my judgments, and do them.* (Ezek. 36:24–27)

God's Word to us is always this: *"Cleanse your hands, ye sinners; and purify your hearts, ye double minded"* (James 4:8). There is no room for sin in the lives of those who seek to fully occupy the Promised Land. There is no room for impurity. There is no room for entertaining any idols or false gods. There is no room for compromising the commandments of God or downplaying or dismissing the judgments of God. God desires for His people to be cleansed and pure in their actions and in their attitudes—in the use of their hands and in the thoughts of their minds.

Walking in Purity

The foremost reason God desires to cleanse His people is so we may walk in purity. We are cleansed so we can live in righteousness, walk in the ways of the Lord, keep His commandments and judgments, and fulfill His purpose for our lives.

Genuine repentance results in obedience to God's commandments in our daily lives. There is no substitute for our holiness as we make daily decisions, choose from various methods and means in solving problems, and resolve differences with other people.

It is only as a people are unified in their worship of God and their obedience to His commandments that we truly gain power. God doesn't call us to be unified in dress or style or membership or any other thing. He calls us to be unified in declaring that there is only one God and one Savior Jesus Christ—and only one set of commandments by which we are to order our lives. Those who are unified in those two areas have tremendous standing with God.

Praise

Praise is the expression to God of our walk in purity! The more you praise God, the more you raise God up in your own heart and mind so that you will want to follow Him and Him alone. You will clearly see that there is no other God, there is no

Song sing I will enter his gates
I will call upon the by

Avoiding the Need to Fight

My *my* *my* *my* *my*

- other One worthy of your time, energy, skills, resources, devotion,
and worship. *my* *Only my Papa God*

I

The more you follow the Lord in obedience that is firm and steadfast, the more you will experience *my Papa* God's holiness and purity. The more you walk in righteousness, the more you will live and move in God's blessings. *my Papa* That gives *me* you all the more reason to praise.

I *I will*

Before you ever sharpen a sword or pull out a spear, start praising God. *my Papa* Long before you receive the things *I am* you are praying for, praise God. *I will my Papa*

Too often we wait until we have received a blessing before we praise and thank God. That's not the biblical pattern. God calls us to praise Him first. Our praise is a forerunner of receiving. *Just like*

The Bible pattern is not "see and believe." *John the Baptist*

The Bible pattern is "believe and see." *for Jesus*

God says, "Take Me at My word and believe what I say. Start praising Me for what you believe I will do. And you will see Me bring to pass what you are believing for."

Include Thanksgiving with Your Praise

A man who knew a great deal about fighting battles and winning them, David, was also a man who know a great deal about thanksgiving and praise. David sang this psalm:

> We are his people, and the sheep of his pasture. Enter into his gates with thanksgiving, and into his courts with praise: be thankful unto him, and bless his name. For the LORD is good; his mercy is everlasting; and his truth endureth to all generations. (Ps. 100:3–5)

Thank God for all He has done for you. Thank Him for everything good you see in your life, your family, your church, and your world. You can spend the rest of your days thanking God and never get to the end of all He has done in you, for you, and around you.

Praise ye the lord
oh praise the lord
all ye nation

195

Here Comes the Judge

Praise God for who He is—to you, and to all people through-out all ages. Praise His name. Praise His nature, which is one hun-dred percent good. Praise Him for His mercy. Praise Him that His truth is the foundation of all that is lasting. As is true for thanksgiv-ing, you can spend the rest of your days praising God for His many wonderful attributes and deeds and you won't have even begun to cover all the goodness of God.

Start rejoicing in the fact that you and God are linked forever through the shed blood of Jesus Christ. He is your God and you are His person on this earth. I'm Papa God daughter

What We Can Expect from Praise

What does praise do in our hearts and in our lives?

Praise activates our faith and gives voice to our faith at the same time. You can't thank and praise God very long before faith begins to well up inside you. And the stronger your faith grows, the more you want to thank God and the louder you want to praise Him. This is a divine cycle—it's like a generator in your soul that gets to the revved-up, fully humming state—and then, look out! God is about to break forth in you and all around you and do the very thing He has been waiting for you to believe Him to do.

Praise harnesses our spiritual energy. Power is not unhar-nessed energy—that is, energy that is random or unfocused. Power occurs only when power is focused, directed, and harnessed for us. Praise is what focuses us for genuine spiritual battle.

Within the body of Christ, praise brings unity to God's people. It unites us as one voice to exalt the Lord's majesty, greatness, goodness, and authority.

Certainly the more we praise God and lift up the name of Jesus, the more we see areas of our lives that we need to confess as sin, the more we see our need to be cleansed, the more we feel challenged to walk in purity.

- Repent.
- Be cleansed.
- Walk in purity and obedience.
- And rejoice with thanksgiving and praise!

God's plan is one that produces your total deliverance and your ultimate wholeness. It brings glory and honor to His name. It builds up His kingdom. It produces all things that we call "good" on this earth and "eternal" in heaven.

To repent, be cleansed of all sin, walk in purity and obedience to all the commandments of God, and rejoice continually with thanksgiving and praise is to follow God fully.

And to follow God fully puts you in position to receive God's freedom and fullness.

Make this the pattern of your walk with the Lord, and you may find you don't have any oppression, depression, or suppression. You may not have many battles to fight!

15

Our Position: Total Dependence upon God

S amson is perhaps the best known of all the deliverers in the book of Judges. It shouldn't surprise us that his story begins with the phrase, *"And the children of Israel did evil again in the sight of the LORD; and the LORD delivered them into the hand of the Philistines forty years"* (Judg. 13:1).

As in the days of Shamgar, one of the first three judges, the Philistines were the enemy that God allowed to invade and oppress the Promised Land. They did so for forty years, which is the longest period of oppression mentioned in the book of Judges. A full generation of Israelites knew nothing but Philistine domination.

Perhaps it was because the oppression of the Philistines was so severe and so strong that the Israelites lost all hope. This time there is no mention that the Israelites "cried out to the Lord." They apparently were so low in their sin and their despair, they couldn't even look up, much less cry out.

God, however, never ceased to love His people and desire their deliverance. In this case, God sovereignly moved toward His people and raised up a deliverer so that His people would at least be at the place where they could cry out in repentance. In many ways, the birth and the call of Samson are similar to that of John the Baptist. The times were also similar. In the time of John the Baptist's birth, the Israelites had been without a prophet for four hundred years. Rome dominated the area completely, and religion had become so formal that the hearts of the people were frozen in ritual. God sovereignly acted to raise up a prophet who would call His people to repentance.

A person may be so deep in sin that he or she has absolutely no thoughts of repentance. There are addicts who are so severely addicted that all they can think about is their next fix. There are others who are so mired in trouble that they have no thought of deliverance—the hope of deliverance has never even crossed their minds. It's to those people that God often sovereignly sends a deliverer.

The Bible says about Samson:

There was a certain man of Zorah, of the family of the Danites, whose name was Manoah; and his wife was barren, and bare not. And the angel of the LORD appeared unto the woman, and said unto her, Behold now, thou art barren, and bearest not: but thou shalt conceive, and bear a son.   (Judg. 13:2–3)

The angel of God that delivered this message went on to say that the woman's son should be called a Nazarite—totally dedicated to God—and that he would begin to deliver Israel out of the hand of the Philistines. As a Nazarite, he was never to drink wine or strong drink, eat anything that was considered unclean according to the Law of Moses, or put a razor to his head. (See Judges 13:4–5.)

When the woman went to her husband and told him what the angel had said, her husband, Manoah, asked the Lord to send the angel a second time to teach him and his wife more about what they should do in raising this son. The Lord answered that prayer request and the angel returned. Manoah asked him the question all parents should ask about their children, *"How shall we order the child, and how shall we do unto him?"* (Judg. 13:12). In other words, they asked, "How should we raise this child and treat this child?" And the angel repeated his earlier instructions.

Manoah and his wife prepared a meat offering and brought it to a rock to give it to the angel, and just as angels had done in the past, this angel called a fire to rise up from the rock toward heaven, and the sacrifice was consumed. Seeing that, Manoah and his wife fell on their faces to the ground. They got up from that position knowing with certainty that God had visited them. They had no doubt when Manoah's wife conceived and bore a son that this child was to be raised exactly as the angel had ordered. They called his name Samson, and the Bible tells us, *"The child grew, and the Lord blessed him. And the Spirit of the Lord began to move him at times in the camp of Dan between Zorah and Eshtaol"* (Judg. 13:24–25).

Samson lived a supernaturally endowed life from the time he was conceived. His birth was a miracle. The Spirit of the Lord moved in him from his childhood.

The Moving of the Holy Spirit in Him

How did Samson feel when the Spirit of the Lord came upon him? The implication is that he felt something stirring deep within him. This stirring isn't a physical reaction—this is a feeling that signals to the body, "I've got to do something. I have to take action. I have to move." This feeling was an inner drive, a motivation to rise up and confront the evil oppression that was seeking to hold Samson down in his spirit—and not only Samson, but all the Israelites.

Our Position: Total Dependence upon God

Some people run on nervous energy—either from vitamins or substances they take, or just naturally. Samson didn't have nervous energy—his energy from the Spirit was purposeful. He knew that God intended him to use his energy on behalf of God's people. His energy and strength wasn't for the purpose of winning he-man contests or becoming a bodybuilding model. His energy and strength was for delivering God's people.

When people are under the anointing of the Holy Spirit, their attitude toward the devil as he comes running at them is, "Come on! You want to fight with me? You'll have to fight the Spirit within me. So, come on!" People who are truly operating under the anointing of the Holy Spirit are fearless. They don't run from the devil; they stand up to him. They know that the knowledge of God's Word and the power of the Holy Spirit within them is more than a match for anything the devil might do.

God's Spirit moving in us is always a signal that God wants to do something, either in us or through us. God wants His people to be a people in motion—always pushing back the enemy, always taking on evil and combating it in the spiritual realm, always being active in our expressions of praise and worship to bring Him glory.

Samson knew what the Holy Spirit felt like in his innermost being. It was an inner drive, an inner compelling force, that he had experienced from his earliest days.

What else do we know about young Samson?

We know that he grew up living in the territory that had been assigned to the tribe of Dan, which was the territory just north of the area where the Philistines had built their five cities. On today's map, most of the Philistine cities are in the Gaza Strip. Tel Aviv in modern Israel, and Joppa in ancient Israel, are located in the area assigned to the tribe of Dan. Samson did not live on the coast, however, but rather inland about half the distance between the

Mediterranean Sea and Jerusalem. (Note: The city of Dan was in the far north of the Promised Land. The tribe of Dan was in the middle of the Promised Land, on the west side by the Mediterranean Sea.)

Drawn to a Woman from Timnath

One day Samson went down to Timnath, which was just a few miles away in the tribe of Judah. A young woman there caught his eye.

Samson returned home and said to his parents, *"I have seen a woman in Timnath of the daughters of the Philistines: now therefore get her for me to wife"* (Judg. 14:2).

In those days, parents arranged the marriages for their children, so Samson called upon his father and mother to contact this girl's parents to arrange a marriage. His parents argued against his choice, saying, *"Is there never a woman among the daughters of thy brethren, or among all my people, that thou goest to take a wife of the uncircumcised Philistines?"* Samson would not be deterred. He said, *"Get her for me; for she pleaseth me well"* (Judg. 14:3).

The Law of Moses forbade an Israelite from marrying a person outside the tribes of Israel. Samson grew up knowing that law; his parents knew that law. His parents tried their best to talk him out of his desire for this girl.

Samson's parents no doubt were of the opinion that Samson wanted to marry this young woman solely because she was beautiful and appealing to their son. The Bible says, *"But his father and his mother knew not that it was of the Lord, that he sought an occasion against the Philistines: for at that time the Philistines had dominion over Israel"* (Judg. 14:4).

Samson found this girl pleasing. He insisted on marrying this girl from Timnath, and eventually his parents gave in to him.

Samson and his father and mother traveled to the vineyards of Timnath to see if a marriage might be arranged. And the Bible says:

> *Behold, a young lion roared against him* [Samson]. *And the Spirit of the Lord came mightily upon him, and he rent him as he would have rent a kid, and he had nothing in his hand: but he told not his father or his mother what he had done.*
> (Judg. 14:5–6)

In that moment, Samson was totally dependent upon God.

What a wonderful place that is to be!

Totally Dependent upon the Holy Spirit

Note also that the Bible tells us Samson *"had nothing in his hand."* I don't know about you, but if I was walking through an area where young lions might also be roaming, I think I would have taken a stick or sword or club or knife or some type of protective weapon with me! Samson had nothing in his hand. Yes, he was totally dependent upon God.

Here is a young man encountering a young lion—not an old lion that has decayed teeth and depends upon his roar much more than his bite. In ordinary strength, a man cannot slay a young lion with his bare hands, much less *"rent"* him like a young goat— which means twist the neck of the animal until the neck is broken.

However, Samson experienced the Spirit of the Lord coming upon him *"mightily."*

Note ~~The Spirit of the Lord makes all the difference!~~

Without the Spirit of the Lord, Samson was formidable. But with it, he was unbeatable!

There are many people who walk this earth today with the attitude, "I am somebody! Look at me. I look fine, I'm walking proud, I've got everything it takes." The truth is, they may look fine

Not you

and walk proud, but they do not have everything it takes. In reality, if they don't have the Spirit of the Lord in their lives, they don't have anything it takes to accomplish anything of eternal value.

On the other hand, if you have the Spirit of the Lord in you, you have everything it takes to accomplish everything God calls you to do.

- It doesn't matter if you don't have a degree hanging on the wall of your office…

- It doesn't matter if you don't have money in the bank…

- It doesn't matter if you don't have a host of influential friends in high places…

- It doesn't matter if you don't have a family pedigree that says you are "somebody"…

Know this

I
…If you have the Spirit of the Lord moving in you, you can do all *me I* things that truly matter and have lasting worth! *hallelujah!*

Totally dependent upon God! That's the place God wants us to be. God desires to be our deliverer, our supplier, our redeemer, our strong defender, our mighty victor. God doesn't want us to be dependent on any other person, organization, or thing that might take His place in being everything we need, every day of our lives.

Have you ever wondered why, in times of need, your best friend is suddenly unavailable? Or why those family members in your close-knit family suddenly aren't around? It may very well be that God is teaching you how to be totally dependent upon Him!

When God brings you through that time of need, you will be able to say, "God got me through!" *My* Your faith in Him will be built up *My Papa* through that experience, your trust of Him will be more complete, and your willingness to take a risk in sharing your faith or your willingness to move forward to a new level of excellence in your life will be stronger. *My* *Every day I need Papa God*

Confidence for Independence

As totally dependent upon God as Samson was, he also lived his life pretty much independent of others. He was a Nazarite from birth, which meant that when it came to eating certain foods and drinking fermented beverages and cutting his hair, he was different. He stood apart from other people. He wasn't like the average young man.

Samson didn't tell his parents about killing this young lion—he was a loner even in that. Most young men would have been bragging for hours after such a feat, but not Samson. He didn't tell anybody about the lion.

When it came to choosing a wife, Samson was his usual independent self. Most young men eagerly waited on their parents to make a choice of bride for them. Not Samson. He saw what he wanted, knew why he wanted it, and insisted that his parents comply with his wishes.

Samson as a judge always acted independently of others. He never worked with an army, as did all the other judges who engaged in battles against enemy forces. Samson was a loner, but he was called to be a loner.

① There's nothing wrong with being the only voice in the room that speaks up for God. *My Papa God is my everything* *7:23 am Saturday* *3-16-24*

② There's nothing wrong with being the only person in the meeting who takes a stand for righteousness.

③ There's nothing wrong with being the only virgin in the group.

④ There's nothing wrong with being the only person at the dinner table who doesn't order alcohol.

Note There are times when we need to take a stand for God even if nobody else takes a stand. If God puts you in a situation in which you are His only witness, then be the best witness you can be!

Watch my Papa God work in my life when I commit all to him. I love you my Papa God

205

(handwritten margin note: pay attention)

Being a loner doesn't necessarily mean you must feel lonely. Neither does it mean you are weak or that there's something wrong with you. Being a loner can mean that you are the only person within the sound of God's voice whom He trusts to be His person in an evil environment, His leaven in the loaf, His salt in an unseasoned part of the world, His light in an area of darkness, a voice crying His message in the wilderness.

Recognize at the same time that God rarely calls a person to be a loner. God has set us into the body of Christ. We are called to be surrounded by and work closely with other members of the body of Christ for strength in ministry. *(handwritten: hallelujah! Jesus)*

Jesus sent out His disciples two by two. He taught His followers:

> *If two of you shall agree on earth as touching any thing that they shall ask, it shall be done for them of my Father which is in heaven. For where two or three are gathered together in my name, there am I in the midst of them.* (Matt. 18:19–20)

God's plan is not for all of His people to be loners—not at all. Don't seek to be a loner. But if God puts you in a situation where you are the only Christian, the only voice for purity, the only person willing to stand up for holiness, then be a loner and trust God to be your strong ally!

The Posing of a Riddle

After this encounter with the lion, Samson had an encounter with the woman of Timnath. He actually had a conversation with her and found her very pleasing. The marriage was arranged, and after a time Samson returned to make her his wife.

On their way to Timnath for the marriage feast, Samson came to the area where he had killed the lion, and he left the main road to see if he could find the carcass. Sure enough, the carcass was there, and it had become home to a swarm of honeybees.

The carcass was dripping with honey. Samson scooped out a handful of the honeycomb for himself and also brought some for his parents. (See Judges 14:8–9.)

Again, note that Samson didn't say a word about the lion or the source of the honey to his parents. They still didn't know their son had killed a young lion with his bare hands.

When Samson arrived at the wedding feast, the family of the bride provided groomsmen for him. These so-called companions were not lifelong friends. Samson didn't even know them. It may very well be that these men were assigned to Samson because they feared him.

The custom of the Philistines was for a wedding to include a seven-day feast. On the seventh day, the groom was allowed to take his bride into the marriage chamber, and the marriage was consummated and became legal in that society. We have receptions and then a honeymoon after a wedding—in that time and place, the reception came first (and lasted a week), then the honeymoon (which lasted a night), and then the wedding was announced to the greater community as having taken place!

One of the main forms of entertainment in that part of the world was the telling of riddles. Samson said to the thirty groomsmen provided for him, *"I will now put forth a riddle unto you: if ye can certainly declare it me within the seven days of the feast, and find it out, then I will give you thirty sheets and thirty change of garments: but if ye cannot declare it me, then shall ye give me thirty sheets and thirty change of garments"* (Judg. 14:12–13).

In saying *"sheets,"* Samson was referring to linen tunic-style garments that the wealthy people of that time wore close to their bodies as undergarments. In saying *"garments,"* he was referring to the outer woolen garments. The wager for solving this riddle was, in essence, thirty complete changes of clothing—a wardrobe of a very wealthy man!

The Philistine groomsmen had no qualms in saying, *"Put forth thy riddle, that we may hear it"* (Judg.14:13).

Samson said:

Out of the eater came forth meat [or food to eat], *and out of the strong came forth sweetness.* (Judg. 14:14)

For three days the groomsmen struggled with the riddle. On the seventh day, when it appeared they were going to have to come up with this extensive wardrobe for Samson, the groomsmen said to Samson's intended wife, *"Entice thy husband, that he may declare unto us the riddle, lest we burn thee and thy father's house with fire: have ye called us to take that we have? is it not so?"*(Judg. 14:15). The groomsmen threatened to kill and destroy this young woman's home and all her family. They accused her of inviting them to be his groomsmen just so she and her family could acquire the wealth of the clothing on their backs!

Samson's bride came to him in tears, accusing him of hating her and not telling her the answer to the riddle. Samson replied that he hadn't told the answer to anybody, not even his parents. She cried all the more. In fact it appears she cried through much of the wedding feast. Finally she wore him down, and he told her about the lion and the honey. She, in turn, told the groomsmen and on the last day just before the sun went down, the groomsmen said:

What is sweeter than honey? and what is stronger than a lion? (Judg. 14:18)

The Aftermath of an Answer

Samson knew in an instant that his wife had given them this answer. And something began to move in Samson. The Spirit of the Lord came upon him. He left that wedding feast before he had taken his wife into the wedding chamber. He headed down to Ashkelon, about twenty miles away. There he killed thirty men who were dressed in linen undergarments and outer woolen garments. He stripped their bodies of the clothing, returned to Timnath, gave the garments to the thirty groomsmen, and, still angry, went back to his father's house. All of this seems to have occurred in one big movement of anger—probably in less than twenty-four hours.

A while later, when Samson had cooled off, he decided to make a visit to his wife in Timnath. He took a young goat as a peace offering between them, and he said to himself, *"I will go in to my wife into the chamber"* (Judg. 15:1). When he arrived, the young woman's father wouldn't let him into the house.

He said to Samson, *"I verily thought that thou hadst utterly hated her; therefore I gave her to thy companion: is not her younger sister fairer than she? take her, I pray thee, instead of her"* (v. 2)

This father had given his daughter to one of the men designated as Samson's attendant at the feast—his daughter was married at the feast, just not to Samson! He offered his younger daughter to Samson, but Samson wasn't at all interested. Instead he was moved to take further action against the Philistines.

Fox Hunting with a Vengeful Heart

The Bible tells us Samson captured three hundred foxes (or jackals), and tied their tails together, and set firebrands in their tied-together tails. Then he set those animals loose in the fields of the Philistines—both the wheat and cornfields that were ready to be picked and were therefore as dry as tinder, as well as the vineyards and the olive groves.

The Bible doesn't say how he caught those foxes, but a man who can kill a lion with his bare hands and run to a city twenty miles away, kill thirty men, run back twenty miles, and then run a few more miles home is a man of extraordinary speed, strength, and cunning. What chance did a fox or jackal have in the entire territory of Dan? (By the way, the same word is used for both fox and jackal, and both of these animals are found in large numbers in the Promised Land.)

Every time Samson captured a multiple of two animals, he'd take the animals to a field of the Philistines, tie the tails of the animals together with a firebrand in the knot, and then set the animals loose in a particular field to run through it spreading fire. Samson set a hundred and fifty fires throughout the area, never getting caught. And meanwhile the territory of Dan no doubt had far fewer predators against their flocks and crops!

As the Philistines tried to figure out who was burning their fields, they decided that all this had happened after Samson learned about his wife being given to another man. So the grooms-men followed through on their original threat to burn this woman and her home and family with fire. The men of Timnath killed the woman Samson had sought to marry.

This did nothing to quiet Samson's anger! Now he had yet another reason to take out vengeance upon the Philistines!

Your Idea...or God's Idea?

In destroying the fields of the Philistines, there is no mention that the Spirit of the Lord came upon Samson. This was a personal vindictive act carried out in his own wit and strength.

Let me caution you: The Spirit of the Lord comes upon a person and greatly magnifies the abilities and capabilities of that person. The Spirit of the Lord doesn't alter our basic personality or talents as a person. Rather the Spirit of the Lord enlarges and energizes and empowers the personality and talents we have been given. This is very important for you to understand. The Spirit doesn't "possess" and alter the essential identity of a person—which is what happens in demon possession. In demonic possession, the personality and identity of a person are changed so that a person doesn't even appear to be himself—he appears to have taken on a different nature altogether. When the Spirit of the Lord comes on a person, a person becomes "far more than himself," not a different self.

There are those who have great abilities and capabilities initially—they may have a great intellect, great ability to empathize, great strength, or great perception. At times, those who have these great capacities and abilities seem more prone to acting on their own nature rather than relying completely upon the Lord to do His work in them and through them. They sometimes get ahead of God or "run" with God's directive without waiting to be fully empowered by God for the task.

Samson knew he was anointed by God from birth to take on the Philistines. But on a number of occasions, he didn't wait for the Spirit to lead him or empower him before acting in his own strength and wit. He didn't tarry before the Lord, waiting for the Lord to show him specifically what to do and when to act. He moved out on his own and did his own thing. Very often, that was to his detriment.

Wait On God's Timing

Don't become impatient. If you belong to God, then God has a plan for you, and He will bring His plan to pass! He has a timetable, and, when His time is right, He will bring you out to the fullness He has ordained for you.

Moses was impatient with God's timetable. He killed an Egyptian out of his desire to help his own Hebrew people—but the timing was wrong for the deliverance of the Hebrews. Moses had to wait forty years on the backside of a desert before God's timing was right.

he obey

Jesus waited for God's timing. At age twelve, Jesus had great wisdom in proclaiming the truth of God's Word to the Jewish leaders...but He went home to live under the authority of His earthly parents. It was about seventeen or eighteen years later that God's timing was right for Jesus to begin His active ministry.

① God is not absent from you as you wait.

② He's not silent or inactive.

God may be using that time when you are "waiting" for His fullness to prepare you so you can receive all that He has for you.

help me my Papa God to stay in your timing

Stay Dependent on God

Don't ever get to the place where you believe everything you do is automatically "of God" or has the full anointing of His Spirit. Don't ever get to the place where you believe that whatever you do, God will automatically bless it greatly simply because you are His anointed child.

Know when you are acting on your own and when you truly are acting in the Spirit. The apostle Paul said at times, *"For this we say unto you by the word of the Lord."* (See 1 Thessalonians 4:15 as an example.) There were other times when Paul said, *"But to the rest speak I, not the Lord"* (1 Cor. 7:12). Know the difference in your own life! *help me to know Papa God*

Now this is not to say that God can't use what you do in your own strength for His purposes. It is not to say that all things we do in our own strength are a failure or ineffective or produce negative consequences. The apostle Paul wrote to the Philippians:

> *Some indeed preach Christ even of envy and strife; and some also of good will: the one preach Christ of contention, not sincerely, supposing to add affliction to my bonds: But the other of love, knowing that I am set for the defence of the gospel. What then? notwithstanding, every way, whether in pretence, or in truth, Christ is preached; and I therein do rejoice, yea, and will rejoice.* (Phil. 1:15–18)

Paul noted that regardless of the motives of the preacher, if Christ was preached, then he could rejoice, knowing that the power of the Gospel would go forth as bread cast upon waters, and that it would not return void. However, for the greater glory to go to God, the motives of the preacher must be pure. Then it is not only the Gospel that is the witness to the Lord, but also the speaker's life. It is this two-fold witness that is always the most effective.

Samson killed Philistines in his anger, and, to a degree, deliverance was rendered on a small scale. But his life did not give glory to God. The deliverance was limited, and the winning of these smaller "battles" against the Philistines did not amount to a definitive deliverance from the Philistines as a whole.

Every time Samson acted out of self, out of revenge, out of his own will, something went awry in his personal life.

Picking Up the Jawbone of an Ass

In the aftermath of the Philistines killing Samson's intended bride and her father with fire, Samson acted in further revenge, killing an undesignated number of Philistines *"hip and thigh"* (Judg. 15:8)—which was a way of saying "viciously." He killed the people of that area without discriminating among them, whomever he encountered and wherever he felt like it.

He dwelt in the cleft of a large rock outcropping called Etam, and the Philistines went into Judah and made camp in Lehi. The men of Judah said, "Why have you come up against us?" and they said, "To bind Samson, so we might do to him as he has done to us." (See verse 10.)

Three thousand of the men of Judah went to Etam and said to Samson, *"Knowest thou not that the Philistines are rulers over us? what is this that thou hast done unto us? And he said unto them, As they did unto me, so have I done unto them"* (Judg. 15:11).

Here Comes the Judge

The men of Judah said, *"We are come down to bind thee, that we may deliver thee into the hand of the Philistines. And Samson said unto them, Swear unto me, that ye will not fall upon me yourselves"* (Judges 15:12).

The men of Judah agreed. Samson allowed them to bind him with two new cords and deliver him into the hands of the Philistines at Lehi. There, the Philistines shouted against him, and at that the Spirit of the Lord came upon him mightily, and the cords and bands felt from his hands and arms as if they were weak strings. He picked up the fresh jawbone of a dead ass and proceeded to kill a thousand men with that makeshift weapon.

That jawbone became more lethal in Samson's hand than a .357 magnum handgun. I don't care how fast a person can shoot and reload; a person couldn't kill a thousand people with a .357 without being overpowered and killed himself—but Samson killed that many men as he wielded a jawbone of a donkey!

After this slaughter of Philistines, Samson then discarded the jawbone and called the place Ramathlehi (which means, the lifting of the jawbone at Lehi).

He was thirsty at that point and he called on the Lord, asking, *"Now shall I die for thirst?"* (v. 18). And God answered his cry by causing water to fill up a hollow place in the jawbone, so that Samson could drink and be revived.

The Spirit of the Lord gave Samson complete provision—not only providing a weapon and the power to use it against the Philistines, but also providing refreshment for Samson afterward.

Note this →

Talk about complete care! The Holy Spirit not only desires that we do powerful work in His name, but also that we be refreshed and have our personal needs met as part of our reward for obedience!

Samson could have known this personal reward and tender care of the Lord every time he took on the Philistines if he had only waited upon the Lord for direction and added power.

Small Victories, but Ongoing Oppression

The Bible tells us that after this incident with the jawbone of an ass, Samson judged Israel for twenty years. But notice this—the Bible tells us he judged Israel *"in the days of the Philistines"* (Judg. 15:20). The Israelites were still under the bondage and oppression and rule of the Philistines—Samson was their deliverer and their judge, but the full power of the Philistines over the people was not broken during these two decades.

For his part, Samson didn't change much in those twenty years. After twenty years of becoming known as God's established judge of the people, Samson went to Gaza, which was one of the Philistine cities, and he a saw a harlot there and went in to her. The Gazites heard he was in town, and they laid in wait all night long at the locked city gate, saying, *"In the morning, when it is day, we shall kill him"* (Judg. 16:2).

Samson didn't wait until morning. He arose at midnight, took the doors of the gate of the city, the two posts that hung the gates in place, and the bar that locked the gates, and carried them all to the top of a hill about a mile away.

Samson's going to Gaza had nothing to do with the Spirit of the Lord. Let me assure you, the Spirit of the Lord will never send a man to a prostitute! Samson was again acting out of his own desires. Even so, Samson got away using his own strength and wit. (See verse 3.)

In twenty years, nothing of Samson's desire for women, nor his great strength and cunning, faded in the least. And neither had Samson learned how to trust God for daily direction and guidance. Samson had not learned to wait upon the Lord for His timing and methods.

Are you willing to wait on a revealing of God's timing and methods?

Are you willing to act when His timing and methods are revealed? *Yes help me*

It takes courage to wait upon the Lord—often as much courage as it takes to act. *help me please am I doing & waiting cause if I'm not please Papa God Block it please*

16

Our Provision: God's Strength for Our Weakness

S amson told a riddle at his wedding feast, but the real riddle was Samson's life. He made the same mistake time after time, and he never seemed to learn from those mistakes.

After Samson had gone to Gaza, he went to the valley of Sorek, and there he loved a woman named Delilah.

The lords of the Philistines came up unto her, and said unto her, Entice him, and see wherein his great strength lieth, and by what means we may prevail against him, that we may bind him to afflict him: and we will give thee every one of us eleven hundred pieces of silver. (Judg. 16:5)

Samson was motivated by love toward Delilah, but Delilah was motivated by the hope of money. Let me assure you at the outset of this story, love that destroys you is a love that needs to be redirected!

Just as his bride once did, Delilah got a secret out of Samson that he had no business telling. It took her four tries—the first three times Samson lied to her, and he was able to break free of the bonds she put on his body. Neither green withes (fresh cords) nor new ropes binding his arms and legs could diminish Samson's strength. The third time, Delilah wove Samson's hair into a weaver's web and Samson walked away with the pin of the beam and the web itself.

On the fourth try, she said to Samson words that were very similar to what Samson's bride had said, *"How canst thou say, I love thee, when thine heart is not with me? thou hast mocked me these three times, and hast not told me wherein thy great strength lieth"* (Judg. 16:15).

The Bible tells us she *"pressed him daily with her words, and urged him, so that his soul was vexed unto death"* (Judg. 16:16).

The devil never gives up on probing your weaknesses. He comes at you again and again with temptations to see if you are strong in a particular area. The devil isn't omniscient—he isn't all-wise or all-knowing. But he's clever, and he'll do his utmost to discover your area of weakness. When he does, he is relentless in seeking to destroy you at that very point.

Confront Your Own Weaknesses *note*

A very important key to dealing with the devil is this: Confront your own weaknesses before the devil attacks your weaknesses.

Many people I know aren't truly aware of their personal areas of weakness. They live in denial or self-justification about their weaknesses. If you had asked Samson, "What is your weakness?" I don't believe he would have had much of an answer for you. It's plain to us that Samson had a weakness for women—a strong desire for the wrong kind of woman—and that he operated at times out of a spirit of vengeance and sudden anger that was not in keeping with God's Spirit. Samson, however, didn't seem to recognize his own weaknesses. How can I conclude that? He kept making the same mistakes again and again! He never faced his own nature and said, "I get in trouble every time I do this! I'm going to stop doing this!"

Very important People who identify their weaknesses are better able to trust God to turn those weaknesses into strengths. They know what they should avoid—the places and situations and people they need to steer clear of. It's only when we face up to our failings and shortcomings that we can go to God's Word and learn what He desires to do in us to guard against the enemy in those areas; then we can trust God to build us up in the inner man so we are better able to resist the attacks that are sure to come!

Note One of the greatest mistakes a person can make is to claim that he or she has no area of weakness, no area in which he or she is more easily tempted by the devil. Every person has at least one area of weakness; it is built into us as part of the sinful nature we have had from our birth, part of the flesh that we occupy until the day we die. The Bible tells us, *"Let him that thinketh he standeth take heed lest he fall"* (1 Cor. 10:12). Don't think you are stronger than the devil or that you are strong to the point of having no weakness! If you start thinking you are stronger than you are, you will develop a haughty spirit, a proud attitude. The Bible is very clear: *"Pride goeth before destruction, and an haughty spirit before a fall. Better it is to be of an humble spirit with the lowly"* (Prov. 16:18–19).

Face up to your weaknesses and failings. That's the only way truly to avail yourself of the Lord's wisdom and strength!

I recently heard about a man who had refused for years to face the fact he was an alcoholic. He thought that because he went on only one or two binges a year, he didn't have a problem with alcohol. A wise counselor at his church asked him one day, "Do you go on these binges about the same time each year?"

At first the man said, "I don't think so," but the counselor pressed him on this point. Suddenly, the man looked at that counselor with wide eyes, as if a light bulb had switched on inside him. "Yes," he admitted. "I usually drink too much in the first part of March and right before Christmas."

"Did any terrible things happen to you at those times of year when you were young?" the counselor asked.

The man replied, "My older brother was killed by a drive-by shooter on the eighth of March. He was not only my brother but my best friend, and since our father was nowhere in sight, he was like a father to me in many ways."

"What about the weeks before Christmas?"

The man said, "When I was a kid, those weeks before Christmas were always awful. My mother went out on the streets to work as a prostitute to try to earn extra money so she could buy us presents. She started doing this after my older brother died; it was as if she was trying to make up for something she thought was missing. My two younger sisters and I begged her not to do this—we told her presents weren't important to us. I hated the fact that she went out on the streets at night. I was always scared she wouldn't come home in the morning, or that she would come home beat up. There were lots of days I didn't go to school in the weeks before Christmas because I didn't want to hear the bullies at school call my mother a whore."

This man faced his grief over his brother and his shame over his mother's behavior. And he learned that he was prone to seeking some means of escape any time he was extremely sad or embarrassed. The counselor showed him from God's Word what he could do with his grief to be healed of the deep sorrow he felt. The counselor also showed him how to respond positively to embarrassment or criticism from others.

Facing his weaknesses helped this man to trust God for strength!

Trust God in Your Weakness

I don't know what your weaknesses are today. They may be related to sex, or to chemicals that help you escape a painful reality, or an insatiable desire for possessions to give you greater self-worth, or to fear, or doubt, or explosive anger. What I do know with certainty is that God will provide a way to escape for you if you will seek Him and ask Him to reveal your weaknesses. The apostle Paul wrote this to the Corinthians: *Papa God what is my Weakness?*

> *There hath no temptation taken you but such as is common to man: but God is faithful, who will not suffer you to be tempted above that ye are able; but will with the temptation also make a way to escape, that ye may be able to bear it.*
>
> (1 Cor. 10:13)

If Samson had cried out to God, admitting his weakness and asking God for strength, do you believe God would have imparted *inner* strength to him? I have no doubt He would have! God may very well have given him a beautiful wife to love. He certainly would have imparted to him wisdom to know how to deal with his anger and vengeful spirit, because God's promise is always to give us His wisdom when we ask for it. James 1:5–6 assures us, *"If any of you lack wisdom, let him ask of God, that giveth to all men liberally, and upbraideth not; and it shall be given him. But let him ask in faith, nothing wavering."*

God will not criticize you in any way for admitting to Him that you need more wisdom. Rather, He will give you abundant wisdom if you ask for it. Ask in faith, and you will receive it!

Acknowledge the True Source of Your Strength

Learn to evaluate your total self! See both your weaknesses and your strengths. There's a great danger of falling into pride if you see only your strengths. But there's also a great danger if you see only your weaknesses; if that's all you see, you are likely to live in fear and fail to take on any challenge presented to you. Don't be a lazy coward!

Note

Every person has strengths. God has given to every person a measure of talent—some have many, some have few, but everybody has at least one. God has given to every person a measure of intelligence, a measure of opportunity, and most importantly, a measure of faith. God has given to every person a challenge and a goal—every person faces the supreme goal of accepting Jesus as Savior, being filled with the Holy Spirit, and following the Lord daily wherever He leads and in whatever way He calls.

Do you know your talents? Do you know your best feature, your strongest trait, your most outstanding quality, your most influential ability? Do you know that you have spiritual gifts as well as natural gifts? If someone asks you to name your gifts, you should be able to give a quick answer, identifying several talents that you know have been given to you by God.

Note

Even more than you must know your strengths, you truly must know the source of your strength. All of your gifts and talents are from God. James reminds us, "*Every good gift and every perfect gift is from above, and cometh down from the Father of lights, with whom is no variableness, neither shadow of turning*" (James 1:17). Every good thing in your life—everything that results in goodness and wholeness—is a gift of God. He doesn't bestow a gift and then withdraw it or give a measure of talent and change His mind about that gift later.

- What God gives to us, God expects us to develop.
- What God gives, God expects us to use.
- What God gives, God expects us to "give away" in service and ministry to others in need.

It is God who anoints our lives and has anointed His Word; therefore, the greatest blessing you can know is to live in His anointing and to speak and perform His Word in this world.

Years ago, we began a church with about four hundred people, and within a year we had more than sixteen hundred members. Things were happening so fast that I had to take stock. I went to the Lord and asked, "Why is all this happening?"

I knew I wasn't the best preacher in town. I knew it didn't have anything to do with my past, my heritage, or even my family name. There were other preachers who preached better than I did. There were other people in the city and in the church who may have had more talent than I.

"What is it?" I asked.

The Lord revealed to me very plainly and with complete certainty that He was the source of the anointing that was on my life and upon my ministry. And He also revealed to me the very specific way in which I needed to guard my receiving and my using of that anointing. He revealed to me the area where the devil would most frequently come at me in order to strip away God's power and authority from my life.

Now I'm not going to tell you that area where I am most vulnerable to temptation—that would only give the devil more power in confronting me. But I am willing to tell you this: the Lord was right in what He revealed! That area of my life is the area in which I need to watch myself most closely.

Nobody can withstand the devil in your place. You must do the standing against him. You must do the declaring of God's Word over your life. You must call upon the Lord to defeat the devil. You must resist him. The good news of God's Word is this: *"Submit yourselves therefore to God. Resist the devil, and he will flee from you. Draw nigh to God, and he will draw nigh to you"* (James 4:7–8).

The Lord Is Always Our Strength

The Lord has been your strength. You haven't accomplished anything on your own power or in your own intellect. God has been the source of every good idea you've had, every good amount of strength and energy you have possessed, every good resource or financial gift you have been given, every good job or opportunity that has come your way. *All Is My Papa God*

The Lord is your strength today. You still need Him as much as you ever needed Him. And He's still as available to you today as He has ever been. *Papa right Now you still is*

The Lord will be your strength tomorrow and the next day and every day until you die. He desires to impart to you all of the power and energy and vitality and strength and ability you need for doing all He has purposed for you to do. *show me your ways will : purpose*

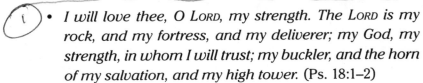

Don't ever lose sight of the fact that the Lord is your strength. Put these verses of Scripture into your memory bank and recite them often as you drive your car or do your chores. Remind yourself of these words as you get up in the morning and as you go to bed at night. Speak these words to your children to encourage them as they go to school or work or face challenges in their lives.

1. *I will love thee, O Lord, my strength. The Lord is my rock, and my fortress, and my deliverer; my God, my strength, in whom I will trust; my buckler, and the horn of my salvation, and my high tower.* (Ps. 18:1–2)

2. *It is God that girdeth me with strength, and maketh my way perfect.* (Ps. 18:32)

3. *The Lord will give strength unto his people; the Lord will bless his people with peace.* (Ps. 29:11)

4. *The Lord that formed me from the womb to be his servant...yet shall I be glorious in the eyes of the Lord, and my God shall be my strength.* (Isa. 49:5)

5. *The Lord God is my strength, and he will make my feet like hinds' feet, and he will make me to walk upon mine high places.* (Hab. 3:19)

The Joy of the Lord

Nehemiah declared to those who had rebuilt the walls and gates of Jerusalem, *"The joy of the LORD is your strength"* (Neh. 8:10).

Your strength does not lie in your ability to feel or express joy. Your strength lies in the joy of the Lord. It is the Lord, the Author and Giver of all genuine joy, who is your strength! It is God's good pleasure to be your strength. It is His joy to give you joy! It is His joy to impart to you His strength!

In Quietness and Confidence

The prophet Isaiah spoke these words from the Lord: *"In quietness and in confidence shall be your strength"* (Isa. 30:15). Your strength does not come from your being quiet and feeling man-made confidence. It is when you quiet yourself in the Lord and feel confident that He is your Lord that you will be strong. It is the Lord who is your strength. Rest in the Lord with quiet confidence and watch the Lord work on your behalf!

His Strength in Our Weakness

The Lord spoke to the apostle Paul, *"My strength is made perfect in weakness"* (2 Cor. 12:9). It's not your weakness that makes you strong. It's allowing the Lord to be your strength in your hour of weakness that results in your being strong. It is the Lord who is your strength.

There is no substitute for the Lord. He alone is your strength against the enemy of your life!

The Strength of God's Covenant

Samson lost sight of the fact that his strength and anointing were from the Lord. He perhaps began to believe what many people believe—that their strength lies in a particular feature of their lives. Samson's strength was not in his long hair. His long hair was only a symbol of the covenant relationship he had with the Lord. His long hair was a sign to both Samson and God that a covenant relationship was in effect between them. The cutting of his hair didn't cause all of Samson's muscles to become weak—the cutting of his hair broke the covenant the Lord had made with him.

For all of Samson's shortcomings to that point in his life, he had not broken the Nazarite vow that had been on his life from before his birth. There is absolutely no mention that Samson had eaten unclean foods, taken alcohol into his life, or cut his hair up to that point—which were the three main features of the Nazarite vow. Even when Samson didn't turn to the Lord for guidance and direction, he did not willfully turn from the Lord or disavow the Lord or in any way speak words against the Lord.

Samson may not have been obedient in the day-to-day decisions he made, and he may have given in to revenge and anger, but he had not broken the most basic covenant of his life. He had remained obedient to the vow that was on his life.

That is, until he told Delilah the key that unlocked the secret of his strength. His long hair was not the secret of his strength—but it was the outward key to the secret of the covenant that connected him to God, the source of His strength.

Your success and strength do not lie in the fact that you go to church every Sunday. But your going to church every Sunday is a sign to you, to others, and to God that you are being obedient to the Lord and that you seek the Lord, the source of your success and strength.

Your strength in the Lord does not lie in the fact that you give your tithes and offerings. But your giving to the Lord what is rightfully God's is a sign that you are seeking to keep the Lord's commandments and that you are relying upon the Lord, who is the source of your strength.

Know

③ Your strength in the Lord does not lie in the fact that you read your Bible and pray every day. But your reading the Bible and praying are signs that you desire an intimate, learning, and growing relationship with the Lord, who is the source of your strength.

The outer behaviors of our lives are important because they are signs and symbols that we are choosing to be faithful to the Lord and that we are choosing to live fully in the covenant relationship He has made with us through the shed blood of Jesus!

In allowing Delilah to know his secret, Samson was opening the door of disobedience in his life—and it was his disobedience that broke the covenant he had with God. His disobedience resulted in his becoming *"like any other man"* (Judg. 16:17).

Don't Become "Just Another Person"

The vast majority of people around you in the world today are disobedient to the Lord. When you choose to disobey God's commandments, you become just like "any other person." You lose your spiritual strength. You lose the Lord's near and active presence in your life. You lose the edge that God desires to give you in living a life that is truly excellent in all ways.

Delilah cut Samson's hair, and the Philistines took him captive as if he was a weak child. The Philistines didn't kill Samson. They tormented and tortured and abused Samson.

That's what the devil does to those whom he captures. He rarely kills a captive outright. First, he puts them through torment in their minds, torture in their bodies, and abuse in their outer relationships with other people.

The Bible tells us that the Philistines *"put out his eyes, and brought him down to Gaza, and bound him with fetters of brass; and he did grind in the prison house"* (Judg. 16:21).

Look closely at those three phrases that describe what happened to Samson:

- *Sin Blinds.* The devil always "puts out the eyes" of those whom he takes captive. He causes them to lose sight of what is truly right and wrong, blinding them to the goodness and forgiveness of God and to the grave consequences of sin. Sin always blinds people from seeing themselves clearly and seeing God accurately. Sin blinds people from their own destiny in the Lord.

- *Sin Binds.* The devil binds us in our minds and hearts just as completely as if we were bound with *"fetters of brass"* as Samson was. The devil restricts our potential, wraps us up in layers of guilt and shame, and shackles our growth and development. He keeps us from facing our own sin, confessing it to the Lord, and being set free from it. He binds us so we lose hope and fail to use our faith and cease to love those who love us most.

- *Sin Grinds.* Once we are blind and bound, sin convicts us and sentences us to "hard time." We just "grind" away in that prison of sin's consequences. We go round and round, living from one fix to the next or one drink to the next, speaking one lie and then another, going from one sinful encounter to the next sinful encounter, giving in to one temptation and then a second and third and, eventually, to a habit that keeps us grinding and grinding and grinding without ever going anywhere, being truly rewarded for anything, or becoming something other than what we are—a blind, bound "grinder."

Sin blinds.

Sin binds.

Sin grinds.

And it is only God who can bring us deliverance.

Renewing Your Covenant with God

We finally see a ray of light in this sorry existence of Samson's. The Bible tells us that *"the hair of his head began to grow again"* (Judg. 16:22).

This means far more than the fact that Samson's physical hair began to grow and, eventually, grew to become long. It means that Samson's obedience to the Lord was being reinstated. It didn't happen overnight, but God was at work through all the dark days Samson was in that prison of the Philistines. And I believe that when Samson began to feel locks of hair on his head once again, he was reminded that God had made a covenant with him. Samson may have failed in that covenant, but God had not failed. God was still in His part of the covenant. God was still willing to extend mercy and forgiveness and strength to Samson.

You may have broken your covenant relationship with the Lord through your disobedience, but let me give you this good news today: God has not broken His part of the covenant. He has not withdrawn the shed blood of Jesus. He has not withdrawn the availability of His presence. He has not withdrawn His desire to forgive you and cleanse you. He has not withdrawn His call upon your life or His desire to use you to fulfill His plan for your existence on this earth.

God still extends His covenant of everlasting salvation to you. It's up to you now to enter into that covenant once again with all your mind, soul, and spirit. It's up to you to say, "I will be God's person on this earth."

Have you lost the joy of the Lord?

Have you lost your sense of purpose?

Have you lost your ministry?

Go to God and say, "Lord, You are a forgiving, merciful Lord. Have mercy upon me! Forgive me!"

Receive the promise of James 4:8 into your life: *"Draw nigh to God, and he will draw nigh to you"*!

Feeling God's Power One More Time

The day came when the five lords of the Philistines met together to make a sacrifice to their god Dagon. The word *dagon* may refer to a fish. Some scholars believe that the idol to this god had the upper body of a man and a lower body that looked like a fish, something of a male mermaid. The Philistines had been sea-faring people—they had invaded the Gaza area from the sea. They were people who believed in the great power of the sea and of the fish in it, especially the reproductive power of fish. There are some species of fish in which a single fish can lay thirty million eggs a year! It would be reasonable to conclude that the Philistines chose a fish-like man as their image of a false god; they sought to rule and conquer from the sea with great power, to multiply themselves and their kingdom over the earth.

Other scholars believe the word *dagon* refers to corn and that the image of the idol appeared as a stalk of corn, which also was a symbol of multiplication and the fertility of crops.

Either way, Dagon was perceived to be the source of the Philistine's power to replicate themselves and prosper as victors over any area they invaded. Dagon was also perceived to be the father of the false god Baal. He was more ancient, and in many ways, more revered than Baal.

Many Israelites had a certain amount of respect for this false god. They saw him as being the most powerful false god.

What does all this mean to us?

Samson was dealing with people who were entrenched in their worship of a false deity. They could not have been more powerfully or profoundly wrong. He was confronting a spiritual force that was very strong; the spiritual showdown in which he was about to participate was going to be a showdown between God Almighty and the most powerful belief in a false god on the earth.

Today in our world we talk about people getting to the "bottom line" or to the "core of the issue." Samson was at the bottom line between God and all false gods. He was at the core of the issue regarding God versus evil.

Every person who becomes deeply entrenched in the grind of sin eventually has to come to a bottom line, or the core of the issue, in his or her life. Some people say about those mired in sin, "They need to hit rock bottom," or, "They need to get to the end of their rope." However you choose to state this condition, it is a showdown moment. Will God Almighty be declared Victor in a person's life? Will Jesus be declared the Savior and Lord? Will God be acknowledged as God? Or will the devil win in such a way that the person is forever shackled in sin and lost to eternal damnation?

My Papa God is my Lord & Savior

No Compromise with Evil...Ever!

The Bible doesn't present any middle path. Jesus never spoke of a compromise position. Good and evil are polar opposites. Heaven and hell are real destinations, an eternity apart in character. There is no place that is "almost heaven" or "just a little bit of hell." There is no god between God Almighty and Satan. The choices offered to mankind are very clear, completely distinct, totally absolute, and eternally opposite.

The popular teaching in our world, that many paths lead to God, is a heresy, a false teaching. It is not the truth of God's Word to mankind. That is not what the Bible says, not what the Holy Spirit confirms to those who are truly Spirit-filled, and not what Jesus declared. Jesus said very clearly, *"I am the way, the truth, and the life: no man cometh unto the Father, but by me"* (John 14:6).

A showdown moment comes to every person. If you are in bondage to sin today, that showdown moment may be right now.

As Joshua said to the Israelites: *"Choose you this day whom ye will serve"* (Josh. 24:15). I Choose my Papa God. Jesus? the holy spirit

Samson came to a showdown moment in the midst of a celebration to this false god Dagon. He became the centerpiece of a victory party. This day of sacrifice to Dagon was a day in which the Philistines reveled in the conquest of their enemies. It was a day in which they exalted the name of their god for being victorious over all the opposition. Surely one of their foremost enemies had been Samson.

The Philistines said happily, *"Our god hath delivered Samson our enemy into our hand"* (Judg. 16:23). When they saw Samson blind and in fetters of brass, they voiced words of praise to their god and said, *"Our god hath delivered into our hands our enemy, and the destroyer of our country, which slew many of us"* (v. 24). Their hearts became so gleeful at this thought that they said, *"Call for Samson, that he may make us sport"* (v. 25). It wasn't enough that they had put Samson to grinding grain in the prison—they wanted to see him blind and bound so they could make fun of him.

They brought Samson into the very center of the temple of Dagon so that all could see him.

The devil binds and blinds those whom he conquers—he sets them to a life of grinding in slavery to their sin. But he very rarely allows a person to grind away in personal suffering without other people knowing about it. People always find out about sin. It eventually comes to light. It's the sin of others that fuels a great many conversations in our world today. It fills the gossip columns and lights up the telephone lines.

The vast majority of people don't want to know about the sins of others so they can pray for the sinners involved; rather, they want to know all the juicy details so they can ridicule the sinners. In so doing, they hope to elevate themselves to a more righteous position. Or they hope to justify their own sin in some way.

Just like the Philistines, the vast majority of people in our world today "make sport" of sinners and those who have been conquered by sinful opponents.

Samson, who once slew a thousand men with the jawbone of an ass, was led to the center of the temple by a young Philistine boy. Samson turned to that boy and said, *"Suffer me* [which means permit me] *that I may feel the pillars whereupon the house stand-eth, that I may lean upon them"* (v. 26).

Samson knew how the temple of Dagon was constructed. It was like many temples built to false gods in that area at that time. The image to the god was in one area, generally called a court or a courtyard. An elevated viewing stand of sorts was built adjacent to the courtyard so all could admire the statue. This open porch-like structure generally had a roof over it, held up by two central pillars made of wood. This form of construction using central pillars placed very closely together kept the view of the god unobstructed by any other pillars at the edge of the viewing area.

Samson asked the boy who was guarding him to let him stand between these two central pillars so he could feel them on either side of him. The boy did as he asked.

Samson's Final Prayer for Strength

Samson called unto the Lord, saying, *"O Lord GOD, remember me, I pray thee, and strengthen me, I pray thee, only this once, O God, that I may be at once avenged of the Philistines for my two eyes"* (Judg. 16:28).

Samson wanted to feel God's strength one more time!

We must never be confused between feelings or emotions and our faith. We are saved by faith, not by feelings. We use our faith to believe for God's miracles, not our emotions. We walk by faith, not by feelings.

Walk by faith, Not sight

It is equally true that if a person is full of God's Spirit and enters into genuine praise and worship of God "in the Spirit," emotions are going to be involved. There's a feeling—a deep, abiding, energizing feeling—that moves within a person who is filled with God's Spirit.

The joy that the Holy Spirit gives is a feeling.

The peace that the Holy Spirit gives is a feeling.

The power that the Holy Spirit gives bestows a feeling.

There are those who say, "Well, I'm not emotional." That may be true when it comes to their praise and worship in church. But I wonder if that is true when that person is at a basketball game and his team is down one point with just seconds to play.

Those who aren't emotional in church are still emotional creatures—they are just intimidated at the prospect of being emotional in matters related to their faith.

God gave us emotions. I believe God expects us to use the emotions He created in us. We are to control our emotions with our will, subject our emotions to our faith, but also to enjoy our emotions, be motivated by them to do God's work, and express them in offering praise to God. I praise my Papa God

Samson's prayer to the Lord at the end of his life was that he might once again feel the strength of the Lord flowing through his being. He wanted this so he might be avenged for the loss of his eyes and bring death to the Philistines who were still oppressing his fellow Israelites.

Samson took hold of the two middle pillars upon which the house stood, and he said to the Lord, *"Let me die with the Philistines"* (Judg. 16:30).

He bowed himself with all his might, and the house fell upon the Philistine lords and all the people standing there. Three thousand people died as the roof collapsed upon them.

More people died at Samson's hands that day than had died all through his life up to that point. And these three thousand who died included the five lords of the Philistine cities and hundreds upon hundreds of other influential, so-called "great" people among the Philistines. God anointed Samson to defeat the power structure of the Philistines in a matter of seconds!

Did Samson have to die in this moment? I don't believe he did. I believe he prayed to die with the Philistines, and God allowed it. However, don't ever read this passage of Scripture as a license to commit suicide. God's desire is always that people bring glory to Him by their lives. God always stands on the side of life. Throughout Scripture, He upholds life, extends life, guards life, preserves life, and declares that death is an enemy. I never pray to die with my enemies. I always pray, "Lord, let me outlive my enemies. Let me be the one to send the telegram to their survivors."

The fact is, Samson didn't want to live any longer. He didn't want to live in blindness. He didn't want to live in fetters of brass. He didn't want to grind another bushel of grain. And Samson did not believe that God could destroy the Philistines gathered there in the temple of Dagon and spare his life and heal his blind eyes and release him from bondage.

Never diminish the greatness of God. No matter what you are facing...no matter the enormity of the situation, no matter the long-standing nature of the sin, no matter how fierce the raging battle to keep you in that sin, God is greater. God is able. God is capable. And God is available. Indeed, He is infinitely more than able, capable, and available. Your problem doesn't even require the most miniscule amount of God's greatness.

Start praising God for the fullness of who He is, what He has done, and what He promises to do!

If you are seeing your problem as too big for God, you need to get yourself a new vision of God's greatness.

If you are seeing yourself as hopelessly mired in sin or degradation or a horrible circumstance, you need to get yourself a new understanding of God's power to rescue and redeem!

Nothing is greater than God's power to deliver you from it!

Yaay!! Halleluah Amen
My Papa God loves me
my Jesus who obey Pape God
Saved me love me and
gave the Holy Spirit that
lives in me Halleluah !!
Today I'm am Bless I am more
then a conqueror thogh Christ Jesus
thank you my Jesus I am being
transform by the Reneing of my mind
I submit to my Papa God his will in my
life halleluah!
      Sunday - 3-17-24
            7:49 am

17

Serving God as Your King

The story of the last judge of Israel is not in the book of Judges—the last judge of Israel was Samuel, and his story is in the first book that bears his name. Like Joshua, who lived hundreds of years before him, Samuel said to the people of Israel:

> *If ye do return unto the LORD with all your hearts, then put away the strange gods and Ashtaroth from among you, and prepare your hearts unto the LORD, and serve him only: and he will deliver you out of the hand of the Philistines.*
>
> (1 Sam. 7:3)

The people did as Samuel said. They put away their worship of Baalim and Ashtaroth and *"served the LORD only"* (v. 4).

Samuel led the people in making offerings to the Lord, fasting, and praying—great acts of repentance—saying, *"We have sinned against the LORD"* (v. 6).

God's response was to give the people mighty victories against the Philistines until the Philistines were subdued and did not make raids into the coast of Israel. The Bible tells us, *"The hand of the*

LORD *was against the Philistines all the days of Samuel"* (1 Sam. 7:13). The cities that the Philistines had taken from Israel were restored to Israel. And every year Samuel made a circuit from Bethel to Gilgal to Mizpeh to Ramah to give the judgments of the Lord.

Samuel didn't lead an army into battle. He led a people into praise, into purity, into repentance before the Lord, and into righteousness. As long as the people heeded the admonition of Samuel to *"return unto the Lord"* with all their heart and *"serve Him only,"* they lived in the fullness of God's promises to them. They *"possessed"* the land the Lord had given to them. They lived in peace, prosperity, and total freedom!

But then, at the end of Samuel's life, the people came to him, clamoring for a king. From a strictly human perspective, they wanted a king for several good reasons. They said to Samuel, *"Thou art old, and thy sons walk not in thy ways: now make us a king to judge us like all the nations"* (1 Sam. 8:5).

The people wanted a king because they could see that nobody else like Samuel was in their midst. Samuel had named his sons *"judges"* over Israel, but his sons Joel and Abiah *"walked not in his ways, but turned aside after lucre* [money], *and took bribes, and perverted judgment"* (1 Sam. 8:1, 3).

The people also wanted a king who would defend them as a nation against the kings of other nations. They wanted to be on equal footing with the people around them.

When Samuel received this request from the people, he prayed to the Lord and the Lord said, *"Hearken unto the voice of the people in all that they say unto thee: for they have not rejected thee, but they have rejected me, that I should not reign over them"* (1 Sam. 8:7). The Lord gave the Israelites what they wanted, but He also told Samuel to tell them in very plain language what they could expect from an earthly king. Their children would be drafted for the king's army, their harvests would be taken as tribute and either used to feed the king's servants or sold to make weaponry, a tenth of the people would become servants to the king, a tenth of the flocks would be taken over by the king, and, worst of all, the people would cry out because of all these oppressive measures, and the Lord would not hear them. (See 1 Samuel 8:11–18.)

Even with this warning the people clamored for a king, and the Lord said to Samuel, *"Make them a king"* (1 Sam. 8:22).

Now this was not the first time the people had sought a king. The Israelites had tried to make Gideon a king, with his sons following him as a king. As we noted in an earlier chapter, the people came to Gideon and said, *"Rule thou over us, both thou, and thy son, and thy son's son also: for thou hast delivered us from the hand of Midian."* And Gideon said, *"I will not rule over you, neither shall my son rule over you: the LORD shall rule over you"* (Judg. 8:22–23).

As we also noted in our earlier chapter, Abimelech had been a self-appointed king over Israel for three years. Those were years of pure misery!

Given this word from Gideon, the example of Abimelech, the admonition of Samuel, and principles from the Old Testament as a whole, it is easy to come to the conclusion that the Israelites were better off without a king. It is easy to conclude that it was an error for them to want a king, that it was good for the Israelites not to have a king.

That is not an accurate conclusion. God wanted His people to have a king—He wanted them to have the king of *His* choice, which was Himself!

There Was No King in the Land

One of the lesser-known stories in the book of Judges is the story of Micah.

This man lived on mount Ephraim. He apparently stole eleven hundred shekels of silver from his mother and then returned the money to her, admitting his fault. She blessed her son for doing this and then took two hundred shekels of silver and gave them to a silversmith. She had him make a carved image and a molded image (from melted silver), and she kept these idols in their house. Micah made an ephod for himself—a holy garment. He also made teraphim, which were idols associated with divination, an occultic practice for determining the will of the gods. Teraphim were also common "household gods"—idols made to specifically represent the people and situations of an individual family.

After making these idols and an ephod, Micah then consecrated one of his sons to be a priest for his household religion. Eventually he hired a traveling Levite to be the priest of his household. This man had all the trappings of religion, but no Spirit of the Lord!

The Bible comments about Micah's behavior: *"In those days there was no king in Israel, but every man did that which was right in his own eyes"* (Judg. 17:6).

This phrase is repeated in the opening verses of the next two chapters in the book of Judges. (See Judges 18:1 and 19:1.) *"There was no king in Israel"* became something of a recurring refrain in telling the story of the Israelites.

Eventually, a group of warriors from the tribe of Dan came to Micah's house and enticed the Levite to go with them, saying, *"Be to us a father and a priest: is it better for thee to be a priest unto the house of one man, or that thou be a priest unto a tribe and a family in Israel?"* (Judg. 18:19). The Levite leaped at the opportunity, took the ephod and idols from Micah's house, traveled with these men from Dan, and became priest to the entire tribe of Dan.

The tribe of Dan, which was the tribe of Samson, became a tribe totally devoted to the worship of idols and false gods—even though the tabernacle was still functioning in Shiloh. In the book of Revelation, when the angel of God states that a hundred and forty-four thousand people from the tribes of Israel are "sealed," the angel identifies twelve thousand from each of twelve tribes; but the tribe of Dan is not among them. (The tribe of Joseph is listed in its place. See Revelation 7:5–8.)

The tribe of Dan so totally gave itself over to false gods and false worship, it was wiped out. The Danites lost all standing as a chosen people of God!

In chapter 19 of Judges we find an amazing story of another Levite's concubine who was brutally gang-raped in Gibeah. They abused her all night, and she died as a result. After she died, the Levite cut up her body into twelve pieces and sent them to the other tribes of Israel, calling upon them to rise up against the men of Gibeah, who were part of the tribe of Benjamin.

A great civil war broke out among the Israelites, isolating the tribe of Benjamin from the other tribes. The war was the result of a total meltdown of morality and justice in the land. The result was a tremendous loss of life.

After the war, the children of Israel returned *"every man to his tribe and to his family, and they went out from thence every man to his inheritance"* (Judg. 21:24).

It was a tremendously sad, bloody, morally bankrupt state into which the Israelites had fallen.

The last verse of the book of Judges recites the refrain: *"In those days there was no king in Israel: every man did that which was right in his own eyes"* (v. 25).

What a sad commentary on these people who had once known the amazing, incredible power and presence of God in their lives!

To be totally without a king is a devastating state to be in.

God wanted the people of Israel to have a king. He wanted them to exalt Him as their King! *My Jesus is my Savior*

God Desires to Be Your King

In Hebrew the word for *king* initially appears to be the same word as "counselor." The word later came to mean "possessor." The king was the one who made the laws for a particular people and who had responsibility and authority over the people. Kings were sometimes the leaders of small cities that functioned as independent states. Sometimes they were the leaders of vast empires.

The word *kingdom* refers to the territory ruled by a king. The word also refers to a king's subjects.

The Israelites totally lost sight of God being their king. They no longer saw themselves as subject to the King of the whole earth. They were neither counseled by Him—which means subject to His laws and judgments—nor possessed by Him as His chosen people.

I always grimace when I see a bumper sticker that says "God is my copilot." That means the driver is the pilot!

God doesn't want to be the copilot of our lives. He wants to be the pilot. He wants to be installed on the throne of our hearts as our *King!*

It is to God that our ultimate allegiance, loyalty, and worship belong. Oh, we can honor and respect people. We can be loyal to a president or governor or mayor. But our praise and worship and total obedience belong to God!

His Claim to the Thrones of Our Hearts

The Psalms especially are filled with references to God as the King of His people:

> *Hearken unto the voice of my cry, my King, and my God: for unto thee will I pray.* (Ps. 5:2)

The LORD is King for ever and ever: the heathen are perished out of his land. (Ps. 10:16)

The LORD sitteth King for ever. (Ps. 29:10)

Lift up your heads, O ye gates; and be ye lift up, ye everlasting doors; and the King of glory shall come in. Who is this King of glory? The LORD strong and mighty, the LORD mighty in battle. Lift up your heads, O ye gates; even lift them up, ye everlasting doors; and the King of glory shall come in. Who is this King of glory? The LORD of hosts, he is the King of glory. (Ps. 24:7–10)

Thou art my King, O God: command deliverances for Jacob. Through thee will we push down our enemies: through thy name will we tread them under that rise up against us. (Ps. 44:4–5)

Sing praises to God, sing praises: sing praises unto our King, sing praises. For God is the King of all the earth: sing ye praises with understanding. God reigneth over the heathen: God sitteth upon the throne of his holiness. The princes of the people are gathered together, even the people of the God of Abraham: for the shields of the earth belong unto God: he is greatly exalted. (Ps. 47:6–9)

For the LORD is our defence; and the Holy One of Israel is our king. (Ps. 89:18)

Let the children of Zion be joyful in their King. Let them praise his name in the dance: let them sing praises unto him with the timbrel and harp. For the LORD taketh pleasure in his people. (Ps. 149:2–4)

The Magnificent Majesty of Our King!

The Bible gives vivid descriptions of the King we worship.

Our King is clothed in a garment white as snow, but even more importantly, He is clothed with honor and majesty and covered with great light, the color of an amber fire (Dan. 7:9; Ps. 104:1–2; Ezek. 1:27).

His throne is in heaven, and it appears as a fiery flame in the brilliant color of a sapphire (Ps. 103:19; Dan. 7:9; Ezek. 1:26).

The clouds are His chariot, and He walks on the wings of the wind (Ps. 104:3).

Our King has perfect laws, sure testimonies, right statutes, and pure commandments that convert the soul, make the simple wise, bring joy to the heart, and enlighten the eyes (Ps. 19:7–8).

Our King has an army—a mighty host of angels who do His bidding and enforce His judgments—and they are totally subject to His will (Dan. 4:35).

Our King has a scepter of righteousness that stands against all iniquity (Heb. 1:8).

Our King has made all His enemies as a footstool for His feet (Heb. 1:13).

What a mighty, majestic, glorious King we have!

He Alone Is Worthy

The Lord is worthy of our praise as King above all gods. Truly He is the King of Kings, and the Lord of Lords. Psalm 95 opens with these words:

> O come, let us sing unto the LORD: let us make a joyful noise to the rock of our salvation. Let us come before his presence with thanksgiving, and make a joyful noise unto him with psalms. For the LORD is a great God, and a great King above all gods. (Ps. 95:1–3)

We have a joyful celebration in my church when we praise the Lord. The reason? We are singing to our King!

There's a reason for the organ to play…

There's a reason for the trumpets to blast…

There's a reason for the stringed instruments to be played…

There's a reason for the tambourines to jangle…

There's a reason for the cymbals to be sounded…

There's a reason for the people to shout and sing and clap and wave…

…The King is being acknowledged as *King!*

When people are stone quiet in their worship, I can't help but wonder if they truly have a *King*. Kings are worthy of a "joyful noise" made in their honor!

Later, when the people came back to Samuel and complained about King Saul and admitted that they had done an evil thing in asking for a king, Samuel said to the people:

> *Fear not: ye have done all this wickedness: yet turn not aside from following the LORD, but serve the LORD with all your heart; and turn ye not aside: for then should ye go after vain things, which cannot profit nor deliver; for they are vain. For the LORD will not forsake his people for his great name's sake: because it hath pleased the LORD to make you his people. Moreover as for me, God forbid that I should sin against the LORD in ceasing to pray for you: but I will teach you the good and the right way: only fear the LORD, and serve him in truth with all your heart: for consider how great things he hath done for you. But if ye shall still do wickedly, ye shall be consumed, both ye and your king.*
>
> (1 Sam. 12:20–25)

The Israelites had no authority or privilege to tell their *King* who and how and what to put over them as a king!

When we begin to tell the Creator how to create us…

When we begin to tell the Potter how to craft us and use us…

When we begin to tell the Shepherd how to lead us...

We have overstepped our role on this earth. We have taken the position that we are higher than God, that we know better than God, that we have more dominion than God. That is never case—never has been and never will be. That is human pride and nothing but pride. And pride always leads to a great fall.

No, the error of the Israelites was not merely that they wanted a king. Their great error was that they wanted a king other than God.

Who Is Your King Today?

Let me ask you, "Do you have a king? Who is your king? Is your king the King of all Kings?"

If you don't have a king, then in all likelihood you are just doing your own thing according to your own fleshly desires.

If you have any king other than King Jesus, you have a false god as your king.

It is only when God is our King that we can live in purity, holiness, and righteousness and inherit fully and freely the fullness of the promises and blessings of God!

Conclusion

Have You Been Convicted and Sentenced? It's Time to Be Set Free!

Let me ask you again the questions I asked you on the opening page of this book:

Are you enjoying all of God's blessings in your life today?

Are you receiving the fullness of God's promises?

Are you dwelling in total protection and provision—in spirit, mind, body, relationships, and material possessions?

Are you experiencing the love and presence of God in your life, without any hindrances of fear, doubt, or other emotional need?

In other words, are you living in freedom?

Living fully and freely in a Land of Abundance and Blessing is God's plan for you. It's the promise He wants to fulfill in your life. God wants you to be free of whatever it is that is holding you back from experiencing His joy, peace, provision, protection, and loving presence! He desires to deliver you and set you free!

Make today the day of your deliverance.

Cry out to God with a humble heart, confessing your sin, your weakness, your faults and failures, your addictions, your doubt and fear.

Ask God to forgive you and cleanse you.

Set your mind, heart, and soul to obeying His commandments and judgments.

Choose daily to walk in purity, holiness, and righteousness.

Praise God as you walk out your life daily, seeking His guidance continually and rejoicing in His constant presence with you.

God is faithful. He will deliver you if you will turn to Him and acknowledge Him as your Deliverer and your supreme Judge.

About the Author

Bishop G. E. Patterson was born September 22, 1939, to Bishop and Mrs. W. A. Patterson, Sr., in Humboldt, Tennessee. He has been a Gospel minister for over forty years, having accepted his calling at age 17. He was ordained as an Elder in the Church of God in Christ in 1957 by Bishop J. S. Bailey in Detroit, Michigan.

Bishop G. E. Patterson is a scholar as well as a minister. He attended Lemoyne-Owen College in Memphis, Tennessee, and Detroit Bible Institute, and holds an honorary doctorate from Oral Roberts University. Bishop Patterson is a contributing writer in the *Spirit-Filled Life Bible* (KJV), which was edited by Dr. Jack Hayford.

Bishop Patterson is a pastor. He founded Temple of Deliverance in 1975; twenty-five years later Temple of Deliverance Church of God in Christ has a roll of more than thirteen thousand with more than six thousand active members. In May 1999, Bishop Patterson and Temple of Deliverance Church of God in Christ entered their New Worship Center, which cost approximately thirteen million dollars and seats approximately five thousand. It is one of the fastest growing congregations in the country. Because the church has three facilities, it is described as "one church in three locations." During his ministerial career, Bishop Patterson has organized seven churches across the country.

Bishop Patterson is a visionary. He is the founder and president of Bountiful Blessings Ministries, which is viewed nationwide and internationally on the BET and TBN cable networks and a variety of local television stations throughout the country. He is the editor and publisher of the Bountiful Blessings Magazine with a distribution list of more than one-hundred thousand individuals. He is the president and general manager of WBBP Radio, a 5000-watt, Full Gospel radio station. He is president of Podium Records, a newly formed record label whose first project, "Bishop G. E. Patterson Presents Rance Allen and the Soul Winner's Conference Choir," was nominated for a 1999 Grammy Award.

Bishop Patterson is a churchman. On November 14, 2000, he was elected as Presiding Bishop of the Church of God in Christ, Inc. He is the jurisdictional Prelate of Tennessee Fourth Ecclesiastical Jurisdiction and a member of the General Board of the Church of God in Christ, Inc. He is one of the most sought-out speakers in the country.

Bishop Patterson has been married to his beautiful wife, Louise, for over three decades.

OTHER POWERFUL Books
from Whitaker House

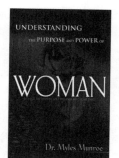

Understanding the Purpose and Power of Woman
Dr. Myles Munroe

To live successfully in the world, women need to know who they are and what role they play today. They need a new awareness of who they are, and new skills to meet today's challenges. Myles Munroe helps women to discover who they are. Whether you are a woman or a man, married or single, this book will help you to understand the woman as she was meant to be.

ISBN: 0-88368-671-6 • Trade • 208 pages

Understanding the Purpose and Power of Men
Dr. Myles Munroe

Today, the world is sending out conflicting signals about what it means to be a man. Many men are questioning who they are and what roles they fulfill in life—as a male, a husband, and a father. Best-selling author Myles Munroe examines cultural attitudes toward men and discusses the purpose God has given them. Discover the destiny and potential of the man as he was meant to be.

ISBN: 0-88368-725-9 • Trade • 224 pages

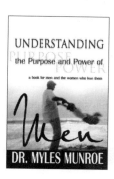

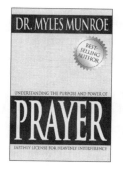

Understanding the Purpose and Power of Prayer
Dr. Myles Munroe

All that God is—and all that God has—may be received through prayer. Everything you need to fulfill your purpose on earth is available to you through prayer. The biblically-based, time-tested principles presented here will ignite and transform the way you pray. Be prepared to enter into a new dimension of faith, a deeper revelation of God's love, and a renewed understanding that your prayers can truly move the finger of God.

ISBN: 0-88368-442-X • Trade • 240 pages

Available at Your Local Christian Bookstore
Visit our web site at: www.whitakerhouse.com

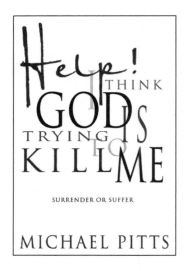

ANOTHER POWERFUL *B*OOK

from Whitaker House

All You Need Is a Good Brainwashing

Dr. Frank Summerfield

You are not a mistake. God strategically designed you with a purpose,
a plan, and a destiny. Your mind is the key to unlocking your God-given
destiny. Dr. Frank Summerfield exposes the tactics that the enemy uses
to deceive you and challenges you to fight back by making the changes
necessary to renew your mind to God's way of thinking. Discover who
you were really created to be—victorious, successful, healthy, and full of
purpose. Take the "scrubbing bubbles" of God's Word, open your mind,
and give yourself a good brainwashing.

ISBN: 0-88368-771-2 • Trade • 192 pages

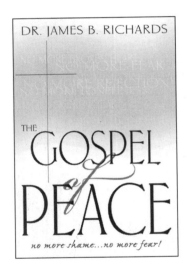

ANOTHER POWERFUL *B*OOK
from Whitaker House

Make Fear Bow
Dr. Gary V. Whetstone

So many times you've tried to talk yourself out of the terror that gnaws within, but it hasn't worked. You're riddled with tension and guilt. You try to move forward, but unseen fears lurk around every corner, causing you to imagine the worst. You're frozen in your tracks, held captive by fear. But life doesn't have to be this way. You can live in confidence and peace. Using time-tested biblical principles, you can conquer your fears and walk in freedom. Dr. Gary Whetstone shows you how to *Make Fear Bow* today!

ISBN: 0-88368-776-3 • Trade • 272 pages

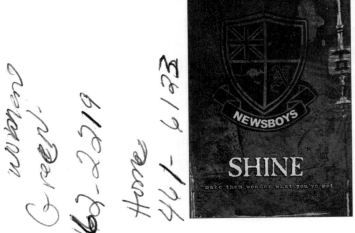